Praise for
Soul of a Dog and Jon Katz

"Like [Katz's] previous books, *Soul of a Dog* is a lyrical yet unsentimental memoir about the bond between people and animals. . . . You will admire and respect his dog Rose, but not because she's cute or cuddly—or, heaven forbid, chatty."
—*Chicago Tribune*

"Few authors are as plugged in to their animals as Jon Katz. . . . *Soul of a Dog* allows Katz to tell the stories of the remarkable animals he has collected on his farm in northern New York. . . . If you haven't read any of his eighteen books, start with the first, *A Dog Year,* and don't stop until you finish *The Dogs of Bedlam Farm, A Good Dog, Dog Days, Izzy & Lenore* and *Soul of a Dog.*"
—*Dayton Daily News*

"Jon Katz . . . continues mining the rich vein that is Bedlam Farm, this time tackling the question: 'Do animals have a soul?' His rich vignettes may just inspire you to take a journey upstate to meet the creatures who call Bedlam home."

—New York *Daily News*

"*A Good Dog* and *Izzy & Lenore* . . . are among the author's many quiet masterpieces about living and working with dogs and other animals on an upstate New York farm."

—*Chicago Tribune*

"From Toto to Marley, our canine friends are a sure bet in the literary biz. But no one seems to speak their language like Jon Katz."

—*San Antonio Express-News*

"We think we know what they're thinking and what their motivations are. And perhaps most provocatively, we have started to think our pets actually have souls. This is the question that consumes author and farmer Jon Katz in his eighteenth book, *Soul of a Dog*."

—*New York Post*

"As Katz continues his zestful, moving, and immensely popular chronicle of life on Bedlam Farm, he conducts a running inquiry into the question of whether animals have souls. He looks to Aristotle, Aquinas, and Jeremy Bentham; muses on the evolution of human and animal relationships; and talks with a preacher; but mostly he carefully observes his beloved animals and assesses the profound joy and solace they arouse in himself and others. In his latest irresistible and thoughtful farm dispatches, Katz shares his adventures with Rose, a serious and hardworking border collie, and Lenore, a loving Lab; marvels over an unusually bold chicken named Henrietta; puts up with his jeering goats; and submits to the blatant manipulation of his "crafty steer," Elvis, all the while contemplating the mysteries of animal consciousness. As close as our bonds with animals become, Katz avers, we must recognize and respect how divergent our inner lives are from theirs. And though we must take responsibility for animals, Katz has no doubt that we need them more than they need us."

—Booklist

ALSO BY JON KATZ

Izzy & Lenore

Dog Days

A Good Dog

Katz on Dogs

The Dogs of Bedlam Farm

The New Work of Dogs

A Dog Year

Geeks

Running to the Mountain

Virtuous Reality

Media Rants

Sign Off

Death by Station Wagon

The Family Stalker

The Last Housewife

The Fathers' Club

Death Row

SOUL OF A DOG

SOUL OF A DOG

Reflections on the Spirits of the Animals of Bedlam Farm

JON KATZ

RANDOM HOUSE TRADE PAPERBACKS ⬤ NEW YORK

While all of the incidents in *Soul of a Dog* actually happened, some of the names and personal characteristics of some of the individuals have been changed. Any resulting resemblance to persons living or dead is entirely coincidental and unintentional.

2010 Random House Trade Paperback Edition

Published in the United States by Random House Trade Paperbacks, an imprint of The Random House Publishing Group, a division of Random House, Inc., New York.

RANDOM HOUSE TRADE PAPERBACKS and colophon are trademarks of Random House, Inc.

Originally published in hardcover in the United States by Villard Books, an imprint of The Random House Publishing Group, a division of Random House, Inc., in 2009.

LIBRARY OF CONGRESS CATALOGING-IN-PUBLICATION DATA

Katz, Jon.
Soul of a dog: reflections on the spirits of the animals of Bedlam Farm / Jon Katz.
p. cm.
ISBN 978-0-8129-7773-8
1. Domestic animals—Anecdotes.   2. Bedlam Farm (West Hebron, N.Y.)—Anecdotes.   3. Farm life—New York—West Hebron—Anecdotes.
I. Title.
SF416.K38 2009   636.0092'9—dc22   20090290152

Printed in the United States of America

www.atrandom.com

2 4 6 8 9 7 5 3 1

Photographs by Jon Katz

Book design by Susan Turner

For Maria,
who always came through the door

THE SOUL OF A DOG

Dog, n.   A subsidiary Deity designed to catch the
overflow and surplus of the world's worship.

—AMBROSE BIERCE,
The Devil's Dictionary (1911)

I F I DIDN'T HAVE A DOG LIKE ROSE, I WOULDN'T KNOW OR
care that a big fat ugly goose had lost her mate to a coyote
attack and was wandering the roads of a small town nearby,
hiding away in a swamp at night, at risk of being eaten by a
coyote herself, or flattened by a speeding car or truck.

Because I did have Rose, word of such problems came to
me quickly. Somebody was sure to call. It turned out to be
my friend Becky, from Argyle, who got upset driving past the
goose every morning on her way to work.

The first line of defense for animals in distress was Annie,
my farm helper, a.k.a. the Bedlam Farm Goddess. Annie, rescuer of many species—birds, bunnies, bats—tried to coax the

goose into her pickup, but the bird ran off into the swamp. Annie told me she didn't know what else to try.

Time to call in Rose. By the end of the day, I had no doubt, that goose would be in custody.

Rose is my right hand—my entire right arm actually. On my farm, the clarion call is: "Rosie, let's go to work." That's all it takes for this ferociously energetic and whip-smart border collie to spring into action.

Rose doesn't play much, or cuddle much. She doesn't even care much about eating, and pays scant attention to treats, rightly dismissing them as bribes. Unlike most dogs I have owned, Rose doesn't crave the warm body of a human at night, preferring to patrol the farmhouse, checking through the windows on the pastures and the barns. She doesn't appreciate being cooed over, or having her belly rubbed. Apart from me, she isn't all that crazy about humans in general; she doesn't grasp the point of pleasing strangers, as they don't lead her to work. When we're not working, she isn't even all that interested in me.

She's always working, or waiting to work; it's deep in her bloodlines, the result of generations of service. Anything that doesn't have to do with work is extraneous to her, an interruption, an annoyance.

When Rose approaches me, it's not a bid for a pat or a biscuit, but a signal that something is wrong. A gate is open, perhaps, or a predator is about.

There's a vulnerability about Rose, even a sweetness in her eyes, but there's no mistaking her priorities. Smart, tough, determined, she is essential, but rarely the dog that people melt over or want to take home. Yet she's a great dog.

She moves sheep, separates sick animals, alerts me to the

birth of lambs, fends off stray dogs, rounds up errant goats, helps the shearer, the large-animal vet, the farrier.

Over our years together, she's proved invaluable not only to me, but to others as well. Rose regularly gets calls from panicky farmers trying to round up recalcitrant cows, collect sheep who have gone through a fence, quell barnyard riots. She's worked in blizzards, downpours, heat waves, and bitter cold. She has never failed to get the job done. We charge a flate rate of $10 per emergency call.

Except for one late-night visit to Salem, where some sheep went wandering just before a snowstorm was expected. Rose stuck her head out the car window, all it took to persuade the sheep to hustle into the barn. No charge.

"ROSIE, let's go to work!" I yelled that spring afternoon, and she came flying. The goose was being sighted on Route 47 in Argyle, a densely wooded, thinly populated stretch of country road. She was a domesticated African Grey, Annie told me; her wings had been pegged, so she couldn't fly off to protect herself or find another mate. It's unusual to see a goose alone; they mate for life. The pair had probably been dumped by people who were moving or just didn't want them.

She was big and white—a good forty pounds, I guessed— and loud. She honked and squawked furiously, one of her protections against predators, when we pulled up on the shoulder of the road, where Annie was already on the scene. Geese are notoriously ill-tempered, and they're hardly help-less: They have powerful bones in their wings and peck with their beaks. But this one seemed more anxious and confused than aggressive.

Unfortunately, she had acres of marshy wetlands for shelter. Smelly, mucky, crisscrossed with vines and brush, and an incubator for flies and mosquitoes, this swamp was a good place for her to hide from humans—but it wouldn't protect her from predators.

It was a hot, humid day. The bugs were on us in minutes. Nobody would have much energy for long, not even Rose, especially if we wound up tromping around in the muck.

Sure enough, the goose, running along the roadside ahead of Annie, made for the water when she saw Rose hop out of the car. This was not going to be easy.

Rose looked around for sheep, gave Annie and me a look when she couldn't see any, and then locked in on the goose. Now she knew what she'd come for. She grasped the mission.

But it was going to be a tough one. We could hear the goose shrieking and splashing in the swamp, hidden by tall grasses. Rose didn't swim, so far as I knew. When I pushed a long branch into the marsh bottom to gauge whether we could walk into it, the stick went down about four feet. No way.

Rose began pacing, looking around, glimpsing the swimming, retreating goose, looking at me. She seemed stumped, glancing from me to Annie, eyeing the goose and the murky water.

In theory, we were defeated. A broad expanse of non-navigable swamp lay between us and this hapless, frightened—and unnervingly large—creature. She was in her element, and we were out of ours.

Rose looked at me, and I looked at Rose and shrugged, as if to say, I wish I could tell you what to do, but I don't know. And I didn't, other than to call her back, get into the car, and head home.

I had no commands for this conundrum. "I don't see how we can do this," Annie lamented, already sweating and muddied. All I could do was shrug.

But Rose, still pawing and peering, loped off down the road, away from the goose. It startled me, but Rose never ran away from a mission, so I waited and watched as she covered several hundred yards, then veered into the woods and disappeared.

Unlike me, she wasn't nearly ready to give up.

I worried about her plunging through the thick underbrush. It can be dangerous for dogs in the country. Rose had twice had her belly ripped open by old pieces of barbed wire hidden in thickets; once her collar snagged and she was stuck for hours until she could chew through a branch. She came home still dragging it.

In a few minutes, pacing the bank myself, I glimpsed her circling the swamp to come around opposite me, as herding dogs do with sheep. The goose was loudly squawking at Annie—who was still hoping to persuade it that she meant no harm—then retreating and hiding.

Suddenly, Rose popped up behind the goose, who seemed stunned and confused. Rose plunged into the water and began swimming toward it. Annie and I stood amazed.

Rose had come along many times when I took my Labradors to lakes and creeks, where they swam enthusiastically; she had never shown any interest in joining them. The goose, possibly also amazed, began backing away. Rose advanced, staying well out of range of the bird's beak and flapping wings. It turned into a strange water ballet.

All I could see was Rose's muddy head across the swamp as she paddled toward the goose, then retreated; the goose moved menacingly toward her, then backed off. Annie,

meanwhile, clambered back along the edge of the swamp—
a pincer movement.

The goose stopped flapping and squawking. She looked at
Rose, looked at Annie coming up behind her. Forced to
choose between this obsessive and determined dog, charging
at her again and again in the water, and Annie, calling gently
from the rear, the goose seemed to surrender. She swam
toward Annie, who swooped down and grabbed her, holding
her firmly against her chest. Rose, almost black from mud
and panting heavily, climbed out of the ooze and, in her effi-
cient and businesslike way, shook herself off and headed back
around the swamp.

At the road, she encountered Annie, lugging the goose
through the woods.

The creature was exhausted, clearly spent, and apart from
some final hisses at Rose, who came over for a curious sniff,
she allowed herself to be steered into a large dog crate in the
back of Annie's truck and carted off to her farm, where she
resides in comfort and ease to this day. Christened Sophia, the
goose sits happily next to Annie in the backyard, eating special
goose treats, and honking intermittently just for the hell of it.

Rose came over to me, ignoring all our praise and com-
ments. She was no longer interested in the goose; that job was
done. She was ready to go back to Bedlam and find more
work to do.

This had been just another job. "What a dog," Annie said,
after loading the mud-covered Rose onto her truck. Yes, indeed.

WHEN I THINK ABOUT ANIMALS and souls, I often think of
Rose, of what she does for me, how I value her, what she
makes possible.

She's not the sweetest dog, not the kind most people want. She doesn't live to show me unconditional love; I doubt she could care less about making a sick person feel better, or charming a small child. Rose is a working dog, the kind bred to perform tasks with humans.

I treasure working dogs, and currently have three—Rose, Lenore, and Izzy. Conditioned to attach to humans, highly trainable if they're well bred, their instincts have been honed over generations. Rose came from a working line out of Texas and Colorado, bred not for looks, geniality, or even temperament, but for energy, instinct, and drive.

Since she was six months old, just a scrawny little pup, Rose has lived on my farm. She was pressed into service her first week in residence—and mine—when my sheep and donkey bolted from the fenced pasture and headed into the woods.

I was alone on a farm in a remote corner of upstate New York with no experience or assistance, and no idea what to do. Rose, even then intense and businesslike, was still a novice, a herder in training.

But she gamely set out into the woods, corralled the animals, and marched them back, and I knew I wasn't alone anymore.

Rose waits to work, lives for work. She watches me constantly for the signals that mean a task at hand, even before I can say, "Let's go to work." She knows the working door—we always head out the back when we work—from the others. She knows which shoes I put on for work, which walking stick I take. If she's in the yard and I'm inside the house and reach for my cell phone, another portent, she'll be waiting by the front door.

Rose is undistractable, indefatigable, a problem solver.

Work is her essence, her animating spirit, and the core of her impact on me. Her dedication to it helps make my life possible, connects the two of us in this powerful way.

Rose is, in some ways, the perfect animal to help me consider the soul of a dog. She is heroic, determined, and her life is in service to me.

I am fortunate to live with some other animals as well, and they all, in their own way, have enriched my life and shaped my understanding of one of the most debated and compelling questions in the long history of human beings' relationships with animals: Do they have souls, and if so, what might they be?

SOUL OF A DOG

Chapter One

DOGS AND SOULS

If I have any beliefs about immortality, it is that
certain dogs I have known will go to heaven,
and very, very few persons.

—JAMES THURBER

UNTIL RECENTLY, I'D NEVER SPENT MUCH TIME WITH ARIS-
totle, one of the world's pioneer thinkers. When I finally sat down with him, I found his essays tough going but
rewarding; his ideas came as something of a jolt.

Like many of the early philosophers and scholars, Aristotle took a hard, clear line when it came to animals and
souls. He exalted the rational being that a human had the potential to become. There was nothing like it, he wrote. A
human could develop morality and responsibility. Since animals aren't widely believed to possess those traits (not even in
our contemporary animal-worshipping culture, although that's
changing), he argued that humans had a higher status, that

human values and attributes—including the soul—couldn't and shouldn't be attributed to animals.

What made humans distinct from other living things, Aristotle believed, was that very ability to reason about ethics, to be held morally accountable for their decisions. Our ability to perceive what was right, and to struggle to do right rather than wrong, was our most distinguishing characteristic.

Animals (and children) weren't able to determine right from wrong, Aristotle believed, and thus existed on a different plane. One could no more attribute human consciousness to animals than to trees.

Religious scholars, sorting out questions of faith and the afterlife, carried these arguments further and codified them. In the thirteenth century, Thomas Aquinas established Aristotle's ideas as part of Christian doctrine, which states clearly that animals, lacking reason, don't have immortal souls. Animals couldn't read the Bible, accept God, or worry about heaven and hell. Therefore, they bore no responsibility for their choices. They were beasts, under our control, subordinate.

Mainstream Christianity, writes contemporary theologian Andrew Linzey (who believes that animals *do* have souls) remains "firmly humanocentric."

Maybe so, but in the United States at least, the faithful are creating their own animal theology. Society's broader view of animals has shifted radically. Scientists' investigations suggest more intelligence and consciousness among animals than Aristotle or Aquinas could have perceived. Animals, particularly dogs and cats, are moving toward the center of our emotional lives. It sometimes seems that our love, even adoration, of animals is approaching the dimensions of religion itself.

A number of studies in recent years have indicated that

the occasional border collie, elephant, or chimpanzee shows signs of self-awareness, some ability to see itself as an individual apart from the others of its species, though most researchers are candid about this work being far from conclusive.

Meanwhile, liberal theologians like Linzey, animal-rights activists like philosopher Peter Singer, and many millions of pet owners and lovers profoundly attached to their animals are reshaping the way we view other species, and are developing their own theologies.

I've been asking dog and cat lovers for years if they believed their animals had souls. By now I've met few dog owners who would consider their companions thoughtless, subordinate beasts, incapable of reason or self-awareness. Quite the opposite—I meet people all the time who tell me in considerable detail what their dogs and cats are thinking, feeling, and planning, and who find the very idea that their companion animals might be barred from heaven heretical.

Anthropomorphizing isn't merely a trend in our culture but an epidemic. Some animals who have not learned to live with and love humans (raccoons, for example) do not seem to be benefiting from this new consciousness. But dogs and cats, who've lived among us for thousands of years and have us figured out, are on a roll.

Though I know better, I attribute human emotions to dogs myself, all the time. It's almost impossible not to anthropomorphize, if you love and live with animals.

Consider the way that Rose, who usually spends the night in distant corners of the farmhouse—I rarely know where—occasionally comes to wake me, hopping up onto my bed to look at me or, if necessary, lick my face or ear.

At first, I shooed her away, annoyed at having my sleep interrupted. But I came to realize that this behavior meant something was amiss. Rose moves around at night, looking out the windows, keeping an ear and eye on things. When something isn't right, she knows it.

It might be a fox or coyote on the prowl, or a broken fence, or a sick animal crying out. Once, a goat had escaped from its enclosure and was wandering around the driveway. Once, a rabid raccoon was trying to get into the barn. Another time, the donkeys had nosed open the gate and were heading for the road.

What is Rose doing when she wakes me in the night? Does she intend to warn me of danger, or is she just reacting to her finely honed working instincts? And how would I know the difference?

Animals generally *do* react out of instinct, genetics, environment, and experience, if you accept what vets and behaviorists tell us. We want our dogs to love us madly because we're wonderful, but most of us who spend a lot of time around dogs come to understand that they love us because we feed them—and that's one of the reasons we do.

They certainly have strong spirits, emotions, perhaps imaginations—the truth is, we still really don't know a lot about what's going on inside those furry heads—but an ethical self seems a human trait. Humans possess the ability to use narrative, language, and self-consciousness to reason, to struggle with right and wrong and make good decisions, to ponder questions of a spiritual nature. These are not things dogs can do.

I've never seen a dog, cow, or chicken resolve to be a better dog, cow, or chicken and work on improving itself. Domesticated animals seem to live the opposite way, following instincts and training, accepting their roles.

Aristotle wasn't calling animals inferior to us. He was saying they were different, not comparable, and that we ought not diminish people *or* animals by assuming they have the same qualities, capacities, and emotional constructs we do. The human conscience is unique in all biological life, and there is no evidence, beyond our tendency to romanticize other species, that such an extraordinary trait exists in the animal world. The fact that that's become a somewhat controversial notion is remarkable.

Aristotle's philosophical and theological heirs, Augustine and Aquinas, did believe, for different reasons, that humans were inherently superior to animals. If anybody in Aquinas's time had claimed that dogs were just like children, he would have been shunned.

Our values have changed. Rationality was an almost sacred trait to thinkers like Aristotle, whose culture had emerged from darker, more primitive times when little was understood about the natural or scientific world.

Rationality was the groundwork for learning, morality, even democracy. To Aristotle, it formed the core of what it meant to be a human being, and the human soul was uniquely precious. Animals weren't idealized or personified; they were valued as workers—or food.

Aquinas, also enormously influential in shaping notions about animals and souls, further theorized that since animals lacked all reason and self-consciousness, humans couldn't be cruel to them. They existed, were created, for our benefit and had no awareness of their condition beyond instinct. The reason to treat animals well, Aquinas argued, was primarily to foster compassion toward other humans.

It's important to remember the context of those much harsher times, marked by starvation, war, disease, suffering, and superstition. Pets existed, even then. Dogs were used for protection and companionship, and cats prized as rodent sentries, but other animals were on the periphery of our families and emotional lives, not so central. They were rarely seen as childlike or as possessing human-style emotion.

The number of domestic dogs in this country has exploded in the last generation, from roughly 15 million in 1960 to more than 75 million today, according to the Humane Society of the United States. Figures for cats, rodents, birds, reptiles, and fish are less reliable. In the past, owning a dog was simpler. They were rarely purchased, often ate human food, and were not generally walked, cleaned up after, or permitted to sleep in our beds. They didn't have human names, and expensive health care for them was almost unheard of. Bites were common, leashes rare, gourmet snacks and play groups unimaginable.

There was little discussion of animals and souls, or much expectation of them joining us in the afterlife.

Certainly they weren't as emotionally engaged with their human owners. Dogs sometimes provided companionship, but more often assisted with hunting, herding, and guarding.

Largely beasts of burden, animals were useful—vital—for pulling carts and plows, for hauling and transporting and fighting, for providing wool and meat and soap. Few people in Aquinas's time had the resources to feed companion animals or spend money on their health care. The notion that they might have human-style thoughts, motives, or reasoning was centuries away.

Now and then, pushing a cart through the aisles at a pet superstore, I like to imagine Aristotle or Aquinas at the mall with me, gawking at the overwhelming variety of toys, beds, collars, scoopers, shampoos and deodorizers, exotic foods and snacks. I suspect both men would be horrified.

What would I say to them if, after shopping, we had a chance to sit on the front porch of my farmhouse, enjoying that comparatively new invention—the rocking chair—and talk about animals?

Having lived with pets for decades, I might point out that my dogs and other animals learn all the time. They adapt and react to one another, to me, to members of other species. They change routines, get acclimated to people and noises, track the movement of anything that might be food. They're not so dumb. Yet I don't see them as much like me. I don't see a capacity to make moral decisions, change their lives, promote freedom, justice, or other human values. The animals on my farm don't have free will; they're dependent on me for almost everything they need to survive.

We don't have an equal relationship. To me, that signifies a great responsibility to treat them well. I can take care of myself, but they need me to take care of them. As much as anything, that reality shapes our relationship and underscores the differences between us.

Aristotle's were among the first known words on the subject of animals and souls, and even though our views of animals have changed—deepening, even hardening—the line Aristotle drew stands up pretty well, I would have to acknowledge to him. Not surprisingly, I find his logic difficult to change.

But to many people, dogs are perfect, loving, unassailable creatures. They can do no wrong, even if—Aristotle had a point—they can do no right either, at least not consciously.

———

RELIGION IS NO LONGER CLEAR about animals and their souls; science is even more muddled. Scientists and behaviorists are increasingly intrigued by animal intelligence and cognitive process, and studies increasingly suggest that our dogs and cats are smarter, deeper, and more spiritual than we have previously imagined. Yet these studies are oddly inconclusive, and I often get the sense that we are being told what we wish to hear, perhaps want to believe. Animals have alien minds, and no serious behaviorist believes they think the way we do.

If you are convinced that your spaniel has a soul, perhaps he does.

There is something very personal about this question of animals and souls, perhaps an issue to be determined by the particular mix of emotion, chemistry, spirituality, and experience that defines our individual experiences with our animals. I have acquired a lot of that experience, and a lot of ideas about this question of souls, more than I would ever have guessed, and I'd like to share those stories, my own experience.

I'm in a good position to contemplate the question. My own soul, my spiritual life, is by now quite enmeshed with the souls of dogs—and of donkeys and several large bovines as well. I live on a 110-acre farm with an impressive roster of animals—three dogs, two steers and a cow, four donkeys, three goats, a rooster and a small tribe of hens, two barn cats, twenty-eight Tunis sheep, plus countless wrens, barn swallows, and chickadees, hawks and bats, chipmunks, moles, mice, raccoons, bobcats and coyotes, foxes and deer.

I'm not sure I'll ever know where the spirit of a dog begins and mine leaves off. I think the souls of dogs and of humans often interact; they couple, shaping and changing one another at times and in ways that aren't always visible or perceptible. That can be an extraordinary, and efficacious, encounter.

Dogs have surely changed my life, more than once. My first border collie, Orson, led me to life on this farm. Rose makes my life here possible. Izzy, my other border collie, came out of absolutely nowhere and eventually brought me to work as a hospice volunteer, one of the most moving and spiritual experiences of my life. Lenore, an irresistible black Labrador, helped me learn how to feel and express love at a time when I needed it.

My other animals also shape my life and spirit, almost daily, though less distinctly. Communing with donkeys, who, like dogs, have a time-honored history and—it seems to me—a rich understanding of humans, is grounding, soothing. Hanging out with Elvis, my enormous Brown Swiss steer, has affected my own humanity, and introduced me to the spirits and lives of animals I previously paid little attention to.

The irresistible goats spark my humor and test my patience. Barn cats have more than once led me to ponder the question of good and evil. Even my grumpy old rooster, Winston, has taught me much about fidelity, bravery, and responsibility.

I SUPPOSE of all my dogs, past and present, Rose may be the simplest to describe in terms of spirit. Rose is about devotion to work, about service; she possesses the kind of independent spirit that helps a human live his chosen life. That's no small thing.

Lenore, who joined us as a squirming puppy, is about love; she demonstrates a fierce determination to show and receive affection.

And Izzy, well, he's permitted me to grow not only as a writer, but as a photographer, and, most important, as a human being. Izzy has changed my life, even as Rose helps define and support it.

I think the question of dogs and souls can best be approached for my purposes not by scientists, pastors, or Ph.D.s, but through the animals themselves, through stories about Rose and her remarkable work on my farm, through the shenanigans of Lenore, who has become best friends with one of my rams, through Izzy, who seems to see deep into the human psyche. Researchers are amassing evidence about what animals can think, sense, and do, but so are the rest of us.

ONE BOILING, sticky July day, Izzy and I drove to a nursing home far out in farm country. It was a one-story brick-and-mortar building, neglected outside and grim inside. Most of its residents suffered from deepening dementia, and many of them were crying or shouting out as we walked inside to visit hospice patients.

Every nursing home is different. Some are quiet, almost serene; others, like this one, are difficult places to be, filled with troubled patients, and severely challenged staffs.

Edith was nearly ninety, and no one had been able to speak to or communicate with her for months. She was angry and confused, repeatedly pushing her wheelchair in one direction, then another. If you got too close, the nurses cautioned, she might lash out, turn her wheelchair away, complain loudly that she had something to do, or simply shout, "Get away!" Even the hospice workers, always so attentive and persistent, had nearly given up on getting through to her.

I approached Edith in the hallway, calling her name. She

ignored me, refused to look at Izzy, backed her wheelchair into the wall, and then abruptly wheeled around and almost ran over Izzy's paw. He backed up just in time, and so did I.

I consulted the hospice social worker, then a nurse. We all shook our heads, uncertain that we could do much. Izzy, meanwhile, approached from one side of the chair, which caused Edith to yell at him, and then from the rear. "Get out, get away," she shouted at him and at all of us.

I was about to do just that when Edith happened to lower her hand by the side of her wheelchair. Izzy, seeing his chance, darted forward and slid his head under her palm, fixing his eyes on hers.

Edith froze. She stared back down at Izzy, meeting his gaze, appearing to actually see him for the first time. She took his head in both her hands, and she smiled a bit, for what was probably just seconds. To those of us watching, though, it seemed a much longer time. It was stunning to see, the perceptible bond Izzy was making with this woman whose soul had appeared to be buried, perhaps lost for good, a spirit no human had been able to reach in recent memory.

The nurse started to weep; the hospice social worker, who'd seen so much, was already wiping her eyes. Izzy's spirit was so focused, generous, and loving that the hallway seemed to almost glow, to fill with light. Edith stroked him with a tenderness that, given her earlier agitation, was breathtaking.

Flash forward a few weeks to a very different location: I had to buy a new truck and I drove to Glens Falls and parked outside the Toyota dealership. Izzy, off-leash, hopped out of the car, walked beside me onto the sales floor, and lay down under a salesman's desk.

After a few minutes of chitchat and paperwork, I got up,

shook hands, and turned to go see my new pickup. That's when one of the salesmen called out, "Hey, there's a dog under the desk over there."

It was true; I had forgotten that he'd come in with me. That happens now and again. I once took Izzy into my doctor's office. He lay on the examining table while I sat in a chair, and when we were done with the exam and the conversation, he trotted out through the waiting room with me and into the car. It seemed so natural for him to be there, he was so at ease, that the doctors and nurses hardly bothered to comment on his presence. He was simply where it seemed he ought to be: with me.

This, then, may be Izzy's soul, the part of his spirit that fits so easily and completely into my life that it's sometimes hardly noticeable or worth mentioning, and that can enter other people's existences, too, and bring joy just by his presence.

As for Lenore, whose soul seems to involve a determination to bestow on and receive affection from any and all sources, she has crossed all boundaries. She gives and demands love from me, her trainer and feeder and—I admit— bedmate. But also from any human who crosses her path, intimate or stranger. And from the other dogs, even Rose, who thinks playing and romping a silly distraction from what really matters: sheep. Lenore, we'll see, even evokes affection from other species.

I think the stories of these dogs, and of the other animals on my farm, will speak for themselves. People can reach their own conclusions.

Besides, I'm surely not in Aristotle's league. I'm a storyteller, and, having lived with several excellent dogs on this farm, I have stories to tell. I want to explore that mysterious, powerful space where animal and human link and affect one another. Perhaps these stories will help people reach some clarity of their own about the spirits, souls, and meanings of dogs and other animals in their lives.

No dog has affected my life more than Rose, or done more to make my life possible each day. No dog has brought me more joy than Lenore. No dog has introduced me to deep human relationships, or woven himself more thoroughly into my life, than Izzy has.

Every dog is unique, and so is our relationship with him or her. We each know our dog in a different way, in the context of how we live or work with them, what they mean to us, how our own lives have shaped our perceptions of them. If no two dogs are exactly alike, neither is there a universal relationship with them.

One of the wonders of the human–dog experience, often lost in generalizations from gurus and "experts," is that each relationship is one of *individual* experience and meaning.

Chapter Two

SNICKERS FOR THE KING

The problem of sanctity and salvation is in fact the
problem of finding out who I am and of discovering
my true self. Trees and animals have no problem. God
makes them what they are without consulting them,
and they are perfectly satisfied. With us it is different.
God leaves us free to be whatever we like.
We can be ourselves or not, as we please.
We are at liberty to be real, or to be unreal.
We may be true or false, the choice is ours.

—THOMAS MERTON,
Seeds of Contemplation

I WAS OUT IN THE PADDOCK, CHECKING ON THE COWS—
Elvis, Harold, and Luna—when I saw a blue pickup truck
suddenly stop on the road below, then back up into my driveway.

Soon, an older man in overalls and a John Deere cap appeared by the gate and introduced himself as Jim, owner of a

slaughterhouse near Schuylerville. "That's a big steer," he said, a common observation when people spot Elvis, my gentle giant.

"Can I ask you a question? Did he come from the Hanks farm? I think I might know him."

It says something about Elvis that somebody merely driving by can recognize him, after having seen him once in a dairy barn nearly two years earlier. Partly it's his enormous size, of course, but there's also his curious, alert, amused expression; it catches humans' attention.

Jim had been buying cows from Peter Hanks, my dairyman friend, and it came time to discuss a price for this steer. He was the only animal to approach Peter and then Jim, to nuzzle them both, and to shy away from the truck bound for the plant.

"Truth is, I offered him a low price, less than he was worth," Jim recounted. "And Peter seemed relieved. We both agreed later that neither one of us wanted to put him on the truck."

Wow. I wondered how many cows had charmed their way off that truck before. None he could readily think of, Jim acknowledged.

So that made three humans, at least, that Elvis had gotten to spare his life or otherwise do his bidding: Peter, a farmer for more than four decades; Jim, owner of a meatpacking plant, and no squish when it came to the fate of livestock; and me, a guy who'd never known a steer before but couldn't abide the thought of sending this guy to his death. Not a bad record for a beast supposedly less intelligent than we were.

Jim came over and scratched Elvis's broad neck. "You are one lucky guy," he said, in some wonder. Elvis gazed at Jim and drooled genially.

———

OF ALL THE CHALLENGES, joy, surprises, and tribulations of farm life, nothing is more bewildering or difficult to explain than my instant and deepening love for a two-thousand-pound Brown Swiss steer.

From the moment I met him in Pete's barn, Elvis touched me with his affectionate nature and interest in humans. He seemed to somehow be connecting with me. The dozens of other cows were milling around the Big Green Farms' concrete barn, but this big brown one came clomping over, stretched his head over the railing, and pressed it against my chest.

Peter told me that Elvis (whom he called "Brownie," in the best tradition of dairy farmers) was the first animal he'd ever been unable to send to market. Still, he wasn't about to keep Elvis as a pet—that's taboo among dairy farmers, feeding a steer for years and years—and perhaps it raised too many questions for people whose livelihood depends on sending cows to slaughter.

Elvis experienced a different fate: Peter sold him to me for $500, with various complicated provisos and understandings, should I ever send Elvis to market myself (ha). That's a lot of money for a steer who won't do anything in life but eat pricey hay. But less than Elvis was worth as hamburger or steak, as Pete kept pointing out.

Elvis isn't conventionally lovable. The size of a mobile home, he doesn't always move gracefully. He trails clouds of steam, drool, flies, manure. He smells. His cow pies dot the pasture like land mines, and you don't want to be anywhere nearby when he takes one of his enormous whizzes. He has no sense of his own size or strength, so far as I can tell, so I have to be wary when he tiptoes up behind me for a snuggle or swings his head over for a scratch. More than once I've found myself lying a dozen feet away while he looks around for me, puzzled.

It was interesting to see how Rose reacted to the new arrival. One of the rules of the farm is that she's present for every arrival and every departure. I believe she keeps a running inventory of the farm and its creatures in her head, a secret map she's constantly updating. So when a truck pulls up with a new animal, Rose is there to oversee; when an animal dies or is given away, Rose watches it leave.

Through close attention, I think, she knows where things ought to be, or not be—even intimate things. I frequently drop my cell phone while herding or walking in the woods, or sometimes a camera lens cap. The next time Rose is out, she will almost invariably approach the lost object and touch her nose to it, because it wasn't there the day before and thus merits her time and investigation. Rose finds keys, sunglasses, even coins sometimes.

But when Elvis arrived, strangely, Rose didn't seem to even see him. She didn't look at him, react to him, or try to herd him. As massive as he is, he seemed quite invisible to her, and did not enter her long list of responsibilities.

Even now, when I go into the pasture to visit Elvis, Rose waits by the gate; if I call her to join me, she sits about a hundred yards away and looks everywhere but at Elvis. It tells me that Rose knows what isn't her work, as well as what is. My theory is that Elvis is beyond her sense of work, her self-defined job description, so she just makes him go away.

In this way, too, Elvis is a creature apart.

I would do nearly anything for Elvis. Sometimes, I do too much.

In the summer, Elvis and his best beloved, Luna, and their

compatriot, Harold, graze on the steep hillside behind the paddock. In winter, when the grass withers, we feed them hay, the rougher, "first-cut" bales harvested early in summer.

Annie, my helper, totes out two or three bales in the morning and again at dusk. On cold winter days, she adds buckets of grain for energy. In between, the trio take in the sun, or nose around for edible grass, or stare meditatively into the distance. I thought they had everything they needed.

A couple of months after Elvis arrived, though, he stuck his head over the paddock gate late one morning and seemed, for the first time, to notice me sitting in my office directly across the driveway, maybe fifty yards away. In summer, with the windows open, he could probably hear me talking on the phone, or maybe the bings and bongs of my computer caught his attention. He lowered his head and stared intently, as if he'd spotted a fresh tub of grain. He was there the next morning, and the next.

I took to greeting him, yelling, "Yo, Elvis," or "Morning, dude, how's it going?" This seemed to fascinate him further, and he began lowing in response. We got into the habit of chatting a bit around eleven. I'd come to cherish this monster, for whatever reason, and I enjoyed our hailing each other as I worked.

After a couple of weeks, Elvis leaned his head over the gate one early fall day, fixed his enormous eyes on me, and launched a mournful round of moos and bellows. Was he in trouble or in pain? It definitely struck me as an unhappy call.

My animals usually are not shy about making noise—raising hell, in fact—if they haven't been fed on time. If I attempt to sit down at my desk before breakfast has been served in the barnyard, I'll be looking out my window at a gaggle of braying donkeys, bleating sheep, squawking chickens, and yowling barn cats, all clustered along the gate right across from my study. Woe to anybody who tries to eat before they do.

Hearing Elvis's lament, I left the computer and hustled outside with Rose and Izzy (I'm forever rushing somewhere with Rose and Izzy, the harried commandant with his aides). Elvis was waiting for me, drooling and sniffing and lowering his head, the signal to scratch him behind the ears.

"You okay, big guy?" I asked. What could be the matter? Izzy and I went into the barn, grabbed a bale of hay, and dragged it out to the feeder. Elvis came loping over and started wolfing down mouthfuls of hay, soon joined by Luna and Harold.

I felt a surge of satisfaction to see them chowing down, especially Elvis, who'd apparently been making a personal appeal for sustenance. I closed up the barn, called the dogs, and went into the house and back to the computer, at ease and ready to work. All was well in the world. No sad cow eyes were fixed on me, no lowing directed toward my window.

A couple of hours later, Annie came and, as scheduled, fed Elvis and the others again.

Annie misses nothing. The strewn-about fresh hay was a clue that Elvis was having a midday snack. "Why is all this hay lying around?" she asked, eyeing me suspiciously.

Cornered, I went on the offensive. "They aren't getting enough food," I argued. "They were hungry. You're starving the cows."

"They get plenty," she said. "Elvis is playing you. You can't refuse him anything."

Annie and I take turns playing hard-ass. With the sheep, I'm the tough one, always muttering about whether they really need the peanuts Annie likes to distribute by hand. But

Annie is tougher with cows, muttering about waste, chastising them for not going outside the paddock to graze. "If you give them less," she scolded, "they'll eat more of what they already have. Believe me, they're fine."

But I didn't quite believe her. A bale or two of hay didn't seem like much of a meal for this crew. Elvis had been pleading with me for food, so he must have needed it. He was hardly smart enough to manipulate me.

Even the eagle-eyed Annie didn't grasp, for a while, that I was secretly ferrying hay to Elvis every day. In fact, I denied it. "Just once in a while," I said, "when you don't give him enough."

To be candid, it's very difficult to look at Elvis—from any angle—and conclude that he's undernourished. But he induced me to believe it. We fell into a secret routine: around noon, he came to the gate, stared for ten or fifteen minutes, then began his piteous call. I came out, hauled over a bale of hay, then returned to work. With hundreds of bales of hay stacked in the barn, nobody—not even Annie—noticed the disappearance of one a day.

Sometimes, I had to thwack Elvis on the nose to make him wait while I lifted the hay into the feeder and cut the baling string with my pocketknife. He didn't seem to mind these swats, or even really notice them.

Otherwise, in his enthusiasm, he'd grab the bale and pull it and me halfway across the paddock while I shouted and cursed. I began training him, more or less successfully, to stay.

Between meals, I visited often, usually toting carrots, apples, or chunks of stale bread, all of which he enjoyed, plus some less organic treats. A farmer from Cossayuna who stopped to admire Elvis shortly after he came to the farm told

me he had a favorite steer a few years back to whom he offered a Baby Ruth from time to time. "He sure loved that
candy bar," he said.

Elvis, it turned out, loved Snickers. Merely unwrapping
one within earshot caused him to swivel his head and make a
beeline for me, a sometimes unnerving sight.

Once or twice, after inhaling the candy (king-sized, of
course), he sneezed, showering me with globs of chocolate
drool. Now I stand to the side while he munches. After he's
done, he lowers his head and I scratch his head and shoulders.

SOMETIMES, in ice storms or heavy rain, I feel guilty about
leaving the cows outside. Perhaps I should usher them into
the barn? But vets and bovine experts all agree that cows
don't need to be indoors, and if they're not being milked, it's
neither necessary nor, in most cases, good for them.

Besides, as I've learned the hard way, it's difficult for a
small farmer to handle the mélange of straw, water, manure,
and muck that ensues when cows spend time in barns.
Within a day or two, the interior is a fetid mess—a mess that
grows rank in summer, freezes in winter, and is very difficult
in any season to move without a tractor.

So Elvis, Luna, and Harold, a black-and-white Holstein,
stay outside. We built a large tin-roofed feeder to keep the
hay dry, but also to shelter them from the worst of the ele-
ments.

Of all the creatures I know, on my farm or off, Elvis lives
most in the moment, his world bounded by hay feeder and
fence, trees and grass, and whatever materializes in front of
him to look at. Unlike the donkeys, he's not a curious creature, not that I can see. He's mostly interested in things that

affect him—the other cow and steer, people carrying hay or grain, me and the contents of my pockets. He seems drawn to life on the farms in the valley below, staring intently at them and whatever movement of tiny animals and tractors he can see.

Sometimes he puts his head down to sniff Izzy or one of the other dogs. When people enter the pasture, I see him check them out and, if he thinks they have food, amble over.

He does radiate a sense of contentment. Since he spent the first few years of his life almost entirely indoors, I like to think that he appreciates the view.

As Thomas Merton suggests, Elvis seems perfectly satisfied with the way he's made. He doesn't seem to miss anything, to aspire to something beyond.

Does he have bovine thoughts as he grazes? Who knows? Unlike dogs, cows are rarely given much stimulation—exercise, games, human socialization, work—that can increase intelligence, interaction, and alertness. Domesticated since foregone times, cows are now mostly confined, fed, then milked or slaughtered. Local farmers can't even tell me how old cows live to be, since few can afford to let them live very long.

We don't bring cows into our homes, speak to them or train them, or take them to play groups.

Nor have cows learned to manipulate humans the way dogs have, to worm their way into human homes, social lives, and beds.

Or have they?

THE MORE I PAID ATTENTION, the more it seemed Elvis had more going on inside that great head than might appear.

Over the few months I'd had him, I'd noticed changes. He'd lost his skittishness around people, for instance. When he first arrived, he backed away from most humans, as if he expected to get whacked.

Now he invariably ambled over to visitors for a sniff and a scratch. In fact, I had to be careful: Elvis seemed so sociable that people wanted to pat him, but one swing of that head could do significant damage. And when Elvis got excited and danced around a bit, you wanted visitors in flip-flops to be on the opposite side of the fence.

Still, he liked people, and associated them with good things. And why not? This animal was no fool.

Plus he'd really begun to focus on me. One of my bedrock principles of animal acclimation—the way I introduce new creatures to the farm—is to make sure I bring them food the first time they see me, and every time for months. It's a principle I first learned in training a puppy: If a dog learns to associate you with food, if you hand feed to him and say his name while he eats, he will pay attention to you, bond with you.

Food, after all, is not a gourmet experience to a cow or a donkey; it's survival. Bring a donkey a cookie every morning, month after month, and the donkey will come to see you as a source of nourishment, safety, satisfaction—as life itself.

Bringing Elvis his king-sized Snickers, calling his name, stroking his neck and shoulders, touching and handling him wasn't just indulging him. I wanted him to be as relaxed and people-friendly as the other animals on the farm.

Food is underrated in the human-animal bond, because so many people want their dogs and other pets to love them out of choice or preference, not for baser reasons. Food doesn't feel personal enough. We want other explanations for their attachment to us. *He understands me. He loves me unconditionally. He needs me.*

How tempting to write the Elvis story that I and everybody else would love: A cow confined to a lonely barn is fated to go to market. I save him, and in gratitude he loves and trusts me. A neat parable. I would prefer it myself to what I see, day by day, as the more likely truth: Elvis is savvy about manipulating humans, much savvier than his barnmates.

He understands on some instinctive level that if he pays attention to humans, reacts to them, draws close to them, lets them touch him and admire him, then they will bring him food and other sustenance, and they won't put him on that somehow scary truck.

Elvis, I suspect, is a gifted animal. His talent lies not in strategizing or reasoning but in just the sort of highly developed social skills that anthropologist Brian Hare writes about: Elvis has learned how to manipulate humans, how to read their behavior, to latch on to those who show some interest or attachment, and to get them to save his life. That social skill is, in many ways, his soul.

Like a lot of nonfarmers with farms, I tended to overfeed my animals at first. I'm learning not to; it's expensive for me and unhealthy for them. I'm still a sucker for the donkeys, if they bray mournfully at me, but I'm trying to steel myself.

Curiously, I'm impervious to the importuning stares of dogs, even Labs, better understanding their blatant panhandling and the dangers of overfeeding. But Elvis had become master of the whiny moo.

It was a couple of months later that Sarah Bagley, the large-animal vet, came by to give the sheep their rabies shots.

While Sarah readied her syringes, Rose rounded up the sheep, moved them into the training pen, then lay down by the gate to prevent escapes.

Sheepherding on TV is lovely, civilized-looking, all those people with nice clothes and whistles, all those beautiful, skilled dogs. Real work with sheep is rarely so picturesque. The ground in the pen, already muddy, grew far messier as the sheeps' hooves dug it up and their droppings got mixed in.

Annie and Sarah and I caught the sheep with hands and crooks, wrestled them into positions where they couldn't move, gave each its shots and X'ed its forehead with a marker so we knew which had been inoculated. Sheep have only one weapon for dealing with trouble—flight—and will try to run, kick, or jump, so this was intensely physical, sometimes even dangerous, work. After a couple of hours, we were exhausted, sore, and covered in crud. Rose was her usual stellar self, holding the sheep in a corner of the pen, chasing down the occasional escapee, escorting the sheep out when we were done. As I did almost daily, I gave thanks for her.

Before she packed up her truck Sarah said she wanted to take a look at the cows and give them rabies shots, too. Scraping the top layer of mud from our boots and clothes, we walked through the barn and into the paddock. Sarah went out to pat Elvis, who looked at her and lowered his head for scratching.

"Hey, sweet guy," she said, then turned to Annie and me. "He's getting a bit tubby, though. Maybe cut back on the grain for a while."

Busted.

I got a ten-minute lecture from Dr. Bagley about the dangers of obesity in cows. Elvis, she assured me, wasn't obese, but we wanted to keep it that way.

Ha! Annie was triumphant.

So I stopped catering Elvis's lunch.

BUT WHAT WAS REALLY GOING ON in my pasture? If Elvis was getting enough food, why was I feeding him more? Why did I feel the *need* to feed him more?

James Serpell, who teaches at the University of Penn-sylvania Veterinary School and is one of my favorite writ-ers about the human-animal bond, knows a lot about anthropomorphism—the attribution of human thoughts, feelings, motivations, and beliefs to nonhuman animals—and its implications for our relationships with animals.

On the human side, Serpell writes in "Anthropomor-phism and Anthropomorphic Selection—Beyond the Cute Response" (published in the journal *Society and Animals*), an-thropomorphic thinking enables us to see animal behavior in human terms, using our own language, our own motivations and thought processes.

The attribution of human-style emotions to animals isn't just about our seeing them as "cute," Serpell argues. It's much more significant, explaining not only why Elvis seems to have bonded with me, but also why I'm drawn to giving him more food than he needs.

On the animal side, anthropomorphism contributes enor-mously to animals' evolution, molding the behavior, even the anatomy and appearance, of companion-animal species, says Serpell, "so as to adapt them to their unusual and growing niche as our social support providers."

What's interesting about Elvis isn't his sweet nature, but the fact that he has done so much better for himself than most steers. Steers are not normally considered "companion animals," like dogs and cats. But Elvis has managed to become one, and is being treated accordingly. Neither Luna nor Harold pay much attention to me, or to other humans. It costs them a lot of Snickers bars.

Admittedly knowing better, I've come to see Elvis as cute, loving, needy, and grateful. In reality, he's a crafty steer who's moved further up the evolutionary chain than most of his buddies, and has figured out how to get the human in his life to hop up and fetch him hay bales, even though he's already well fed, even though the human has many better things to do. Not only that, but other humans, with the exception of real farmers, think the whole thing's adorable.

Pet keeping is odd—Serpell calls it "an anomalous activity"—from an evolutionary standpoint. It's easy to see why we raise sheep or chickens or pigs, who pay their way in wool, eggs, meat, and hides. But why, he asks, do we need Siamese cats or miniature schnauzers? Or, he might have added, giant steers who drool and consume staggering amounts of hay?

Pets are expensive; they belong to a different species; they can't remember or return past favors or debts; they may even bite or scratch.

And Elvis is a particularly burdensome pet, if you can call him that. Rose earns her keep every day. Izzy is my companion on the farm. Even the affable donkeys play a useful role, guarding the sheep from coyotes and the chickens from foxes. Elvis makes no such contribution.

Yet I have seen him, from the first, as a steer with spiritual dimensions, perhaps even a soul. So, obviously this relationship does something that *I* need, that's beneficial to me.

Actually, it does a number of things, as researchers have found. Pet owners are more resistant to the stressful effects of trauma and "negative life events." They have fewer health problems and go to the doctor less often than non–pet owners. The acquisition of pets, studies show, often results in less stress, lower blood pressure, and longer life spans.

Moreover, pets represent a form of social support. Different researchers define this term differently, but in general, "social support" is whatever leads people to believe that they're cared for, that they're loved and valued, that they're connected to others and have the ability to nurture and protect them in turn.

For humans, social support is critically important, as has been acknowledged throughout human history, notes Serpell. A relationship in which a person believes that he is cared for, loved, esteemed, part of a network of mutual obligations, is helpful to him, both physically and emotionally.

"The socially supportive potential of pets," Serpell writes, "should therefore hinge on their ability to produce similar effects by behaving in ways that make their owners believe that the animal cares for and loves them, holds them in high esteem, and depends on them for care and protection."

Serpell's analysis, a big idea that speaks to the lives of millions of animal lovers, was revelatory for me. I was reading about Elvis, understanding with sudden and belated clarity why I was dragging hay to him in the middle of the day.

It seemed good for him, at least at first, but it was even better for me. It let me believe that Elvis cared for me, that he was more attached to me than to any other human, even Annie, and that he depended on me.

Elvis had somehow come to grasp what my dogs, and so many dogs, rely on: Because humans often feel isolated and undervalued, the prospect of unconditional love, the sense of being needed, the opportunity to be affectionate and compassionate, not only *feels* good to me, it *is* good for me. And

good for the animals who maneuver, and perhaps even strate-
gize in some primal, instinctive way, to keep those impulses
alive in us. This is the reason we love dogs so much and treat
them so well.

Elvis is nothing if not a good learner. His head still ap-
pears over the gate around noon, he still fixes those huge
brown eyes on me and moos mournfully. Hey, it's worth a try.
I continue to greet him in return, saying hi, calling his name.

After the vet visit, though, there were no more noon hay
runs.

I understood that I was being manipulated. I understood
that Elvis was acting not out of need but opportunistically,
though instinctively. I was, after all, a human and Elvis was a
large and dumb beast—just not as simple as I'd thought.

"The hell with you," I shouted from the study one frosty
January day. "You're not getting any more hay." But I went
out anyway with a huge Snickers bar.

It was cold. I thought he might need the energy.

Chapter Three

HENRIETTA, HEN OF ENTITLEMENT

To me, animals have all the traits indicative of soul.
For soul is not something we can see or measure. . . .
No one can prove that animals have souls. Asking for
proof would be like demanding proof that I love my
wife and children, or wanting me to prove that
Handel's *Messiah* is a glorious masterpiece of music.
Some truths simply cannot be demonstrated. But if
we open our hearts to other creatures and allow
ourselves to sympathize with their joys and struggles,
we will find they have the power to touch and
transform us. There is an inwardness in other creatures
that awakens what is innermost in ourselves.

—THE REVEREND GARY KOWALSKI,
The Souls of Animals

FIRST A WORD ABOUT HENRIETTA'S LINEAGE. HER MOTHER
is one of my hens, a tawny variety known as a Buff Or-
pington, a none-too-bright eating and pecking (and, on oc-

casion, laying) machine. If this chicken has a soul, personality, or identity beyond scratching for bugs and birdseed, it's not apparent to me.

Her father, on the other hand, is a major figure hereabouts. Winston, a big, speckled rooster, was injured on a neighboring farm in the line of duty, defending his hens against a hawk attack. For his troubles, Winston's left leg was mangled, and he hobbles on it like a proud veteran.

A serious rooster who crows at odd times for no apparent reason, he isn't nasty or violent, like some, but keeps a close eye on his hens, racing over (he can move pretty fast, even with his bad leg) if there's any trouble. When a visiting beagle rushed out of a car and headed for one of the hens last summer, Winston came hurtling across the barnyard before the dog could get too close. Like some demonic fury, the rooster was crowing and clamoring, wings outstretched, all puffed up and ready for battle.

I joke that Winston and I may end up together in a South Florida trailer park one day, hobbling around and taking in the sun. I also remind myself that it's not that much of a joke.

TWO YEARS AGO I found Winston near death, lying stiffly on the concrete floor of the barn in deep winter. I went to get my rifle, intending to put him out of his misery, and my friend Peter Hanks, dairy farmer, set off to fetch his ax. "You don't waste a bullet on a chicken," he explained. But Annie, my helper and a true animal lover, swept the frozen Winston into her arms, fed him soup and potions, installed hay beds and heatlamps, and restored him to health. Now he's not only alive, but a proud dad.

Henrietta hatched last summer. From the half dozen eggs

her mother was sitting on (the hen had hidden away in the garden, and it was some time before we found her), Henrietta was the only hatchling.

Annie promptly whisked her and her squawking mother out of the garden and into the tiny old milkhouse, installing a heatlamp, waterer, and generous supplies of corn, grain, vitamins, and special baby-chick feed.

Annie intended to keep Henrietta in the nursery, as I called it, for a year or so. She was concerned about Mother, the barn cat, who'd been eyeing the chick lustfully for days. Mother is sweet and agreeable, as long as you aren't a chipmunk, squirrel, mole, rat, or mouse, all of which she stalks. Their dismembered corpses litter the grounds.

But Mother shares the barn amicably with the chickens; they apparently enjoy some sort of exemption. Besides, I've learned the hard way that chickens are tougher than they look. Maybe Winston had persuaded Mother that coexistence was the wisest course.

So Annie and I squabbled about when Henrietta could leave the milkhouse. In the time-honored tradition of men pushing their kids out to make their way, I argued that Henrietta was ready to take on the world, or at least the barnyard. Annie reluctantly agreed.

We put heavy gloves on and tackled the outraged, squawking mom until we got her chick out into the barn. Annie outfitted one of the stalls with a feeder, water, and nesting box.

Mother circled the newcomers but somehow categorized Henrietta correctly—"chicken"—and both she and Annie relaxed. As for Henrietta, she greatly relished her newfound freedom, scuttling past Mother and outside into the barnyard, where she pushed the sheep and donkeys aside and went to work, pecking at spilled hay and feed, seeking out the good stuff.

The animal population is in constant flux here, as newcomers and departees change the character of the place. Carol, my first donkey, was a major presence until she died suddenly at the onset of our second winter here. So was Orson, my first border collie, whom I sorrowfully put down the following summer.

When Jeannette, the oldest donkey, joined the clan, she seemed to immediately take charge, dominating the barnyard with her noisy bray, unquenchable appetite, and pushy ways. "Bossy boots," Annie huffed, as Jeannette routinely elbowed the others aside while Annie attempted to distribute carrots and brush the donkeys' shaggy coats. (They eventually reached an accommodation.) Myself, I'd call Rose the farm's most dominant creature. But early last winter, just after she emerged from protective custody, I began to notice that Henrietta was different. Chickens are highly predictable creatures, usually—I can't recall one surprising me before—but this one was strange.

WHAT CAN I SAY about chickens?

I admire them because they're industrious, always busy—the only truly useful creatures on the farm. They eat bugs and ticks; they supply our eggs; and if they're not too complex or expressive, that's fine with me.

At first light, accompanied by imperial bugling from Winston, they march purposefully out of the barn and make their regular circuit: They hoover up the scattered seed beneath the bird feeder, then try to raid Mother's dish of dry cat food, then circle the farmhouse, pecking for grubs, worms, and other things I can't see.

They march up the pasture and then down, over to the hay feeder and around again, covering a lot of ground, all the while muttering and exclaiming, perhaps critiquing the menu.

Chickens don't seem bright to me, but, like most animals, they're smart about food. When they see me opening a can of birdseed, or bringing them bread crumbs, they come toddling over at full speed. When they see Annie, they come squawking double-time, as they've learned that her pockets are filled with treats.

They appreciate dietary supplements—stale bread, cold spaghetti, the bits of potato chips from the bottom of the bag, and leftover homemade chili. But nothing slows their rounds for long. They're unfazed by nearly everything—cows, donkeys, dogs, me.

Winston, venerable and proud, sometimes accompanies the hens and sometimes sits off by himself, keeping an eye on things. He is the only animal on the farm, other than Rose, who ever got close to Orson. The two of them often sat side by side, napping or taking in the view. Sometimes, I see Winston up the hill near Orson's grave and wonder if he's visiting.

At dusk, led by Winston, the chickens all file into the barn, fuss a bit, then hop onto their roosts and veg out.

The hens lay an egg apiece every other day or so—unless it's too hot or too cold. Or they're too old. Or something has been moved around. Simple organisms, they aren't picky or demanding. Creatures of habit and devotees of routine, they rarely cause trouble and are surprisingly self-sufficient.

So it came as a surprise to see young Henrietta flap her

wings one December day and hop right up onto Jeannette's broad back. Jeannette can be grumpy about assaults on her dignity or invasions of her space (just try taking her temperature with a rectal thermometer), but she seemed to enjoy hosting Henrietta. At least she took no action to shake her off. This practice continued.

Sometimes Henrietta, who carries Winston's speckled gray coloring, pecked away at bugs or specks of hay and dried manure that collected on Jeannette's back. Sometimes she just soaked up the warmth of her shaggy fur and dozed, or surveyed the barnyard.

I looked up at various times to see Henrietta aboard other animals—a good-natured ewe known only as Number 57, the older ewe named Paula, enormous Elvis, and his daintier companion, Luna.

Henrietta carried herself differently from the other hens. Perhaps because of her status as Winston's only child, she had an air of entitlement, a willingness to be apart from the flock and to do things other chickens don't.

I looked out my study window one morning to see Henrietta amid the huddle of the sheep around the hay feeder, perched atop the bale as the sheep munched away.

The other hens pay absolutely no attention to my dogs. But Henrietta marched right up to Izzy one afternoon as he lay quietly outside the pasture gate and peered down quizzically, staring at him for so long that he grew unnerved. Unlike Rose, Izzy has no ambition to run a farm and no taste for conflict with any creature. He got up and skittered off.

NOTHING MUCH on the farm happens without Rose's scrutiny or approval. She's always watching, constantly taking inventory. If a ewe drifts out of sight, Rose will seek her out; if a

lamb is lying up in the field by herself, Rose will go investigate. My name might be on the deed, but the farm is clearly
Rose's place.

So it was only a matter of hours before Rose noticed this
strange new chicken behavior. Henrietta was settled comfort-
ably aboard Number 57, and when Rose came outdoors, she
did a double take. Rose has a manual in her head at all times
for how sheep are supposed to behave and where they are
supposed to be. Clearly, no chicken is mentioned in the reg-
ulations. She shot over to chase the chicken away.

Number 57, who has known Rose for several years now,
bolted toward the flock, just up the hill. The young hen
squawked and shrieked—she made a strangely high-pitched
sound, almost like a turkey—and then hopped down to the
ground.

Rose dislikes deviations from the ordinary, especially when
they happen without her knowledge or consent. "Whoa,
Rosie," I yelled, from a few feet away. "Leave her alone."

Normally, when Rose gives a chicken—or anything—her
famous piercing border collie "eye," the animal moves. But
Henrietta merely looked indignant, stalked over to Rose, and
got in her face, clucking and squeaking like a rubber toy.

I doubted the outcome of this face-off would be good
news for Henrietta, but I'd also learned over the years to trust
Rose, who as a rule didn't injure other living things (except
for belligerent rams and the occasional small bat she pulled
out of the night air). Nor did she back down.

As Rose stared, poised to move, Henrietta flounced
around behind her and simply sat down on the ground. Now
Rose was truly befuddled. Henrietta settled in, complaining
still about the loss of her woolly resting place; then she closed
her eyes and went to sleep. Winston came lurching over to

see if there was trouble, but he and Rose had a longtime understanding and never messed with each other.

So Rose backed up a few feet, still staring at Henrietta, perhaps wondering, as I was, exactly what this odd bird was up to.

Rose paused for a few seconds, then skirted Henrietta and went off to push the sheep around. I told Paula later that I'd encountered my first empowered hen.

THIS *WAS* ONE UNUSUAL HEN. One morning as I brought Mother a can of cat food (though she found plenty of rodents to kill, she was more likely to present them to me as trophies than to actually eat them, so I still fed her), Henrietta watched me intently. Then before Mother could have more than a mouthful, she quickly swooped over to Mother's bowl. I half expected Henrietta's speckled head to join the next delivery of body parts deposited at the back door, but, to my surprise, Mother backed off. A moment later, Henrietta hustled her right out of the barn.

I surveyed the farmers I knew: Had they ever known a chicken who rode on donkeys or sheep, or who pushed a barn cat right off her bowl? They were unanimous: Never.

Ordinarily, I'd fall solidly in the chickens-don't-have-souls camp. I might land there yet. But Henrietta certainly had an animating spirit.

Day by day, her distinct personality slowly emerged as she evolved from a protected chick to an imperious hen. She was curious, explorative, alert, experimentally inclined, and fearless.

I don't know if Henrietta understood how different she was from others of her kind, nor did it matter all that much. It was enough to enjoy her funny, beguiling presence.

STILL, the question lingers: Did she have a personality? A consciousness? Did she choose in some instinctual or other way to behave differently? Is self-awareness a uniquely human attribute, or can other animals, like Henrietta, also develop a sense of self?

Hard to say, conclude researchers Marc Bekoff and Paul Sherman, professors of ecology and evolutionary biology at the University of Colorado in Boulder. "Although laypersons and researchers from many disciplines have long been interested in animal self-knowledge, few unambiguous conclusions are available," they wrote in a paper titled "Reflections on Animal Selves."

In social animals, they note, the demands of living—cooperation, competition, the maintenance of bonds, and the avoidance of being cheated or bested—have fostered increased mental intricacy.

And chickens *are* social animals. They travel together, co-exist with larger, more dominant species, and have to find ways to evade or defend against numerous predators—foxes, coyotes, badgers, raccoons, hawks. Cats. Dogs. Humans.

Of course, multiple explanations are possible for my feisty hen. Winston navigated the farm with great confidence and skill, so perhaps Henrietta inherited his boldness. She was also the first chicken to be born on the farm. Perhaps because she grew up here, and the other animals were familiar to her from the first, she had less fear of them.

So she immediately took advantage of their presence, hopping onto a ewe on a cold morning and nestling into five inches of cozy fleece. I believe the other hens would have frozen to death before thinking to do that.

The animals' backs also provided tasty buffets; Henrietta

found lots of good stuff to eat there, from bits of hay and grain to parasites and smudges of manure.

If any other animal had tried to ride Jeannette, it would have gotten kicked halfway to Vermont. Why didn't the donkeys mind Henrietta? What did they and the sheep pick up from her that caused them to accept her? I chalked it up to her confidence: Henrietta acted as if she belonged everywhere, and perhaps that made it so.

Researchers say animals "know" they are similar to, but distinct from, others of the same species. For example, they rarely try to mate with another species (although I have seen new lambs nursing from donkeys). They travel as a coordinated unit, without collisions. But, Bekoff and Sherman concede, "There is no agreed-upon, objective way to assess the degree of self-cognizance of an individual."

I wondered too, why the other chickens didn't notice—and adopt—Henrietta's innovative warming and feeding techniques. They seemed utterly unaware of her individuality.

Contrast these birds with Rose, whose animating spirit is so much more evident. Henrietta, however amusing, didn't function at anywhere near that level.

While it's equally impossible to say just what's going on inside her head, it seems almost inconceivable to me, watching Rose work—day after day, on my farm and others, for years now—that she doesn't have a sense of herself as different from other animals, and of the others as distinct from one another.

She treats sheep differently from donkeys. She won't herd, or even notice, a hulking steer, correctly assessing that he can't be herded and that it would be folly to try. Her presence, authority, and work ethic are all distinct traits; she seems to grasp her role in the complex social system of a farm.

EVERY NIGHT before bed, Rose and I make the final rounds of the farm. I bring a powerful lamp whose beam can reach all the way to the top of the pasture. Rose and I have made these bed checks literally a thousand times by now, so we know the drill. We can both sense anything out of the ordinary—a donkey in the wrong place, an urgent bleat from a ewe or lamb.

I pull on a jacket. Rose heads for the door. I check my cell phone; sometimes I have needed it out there at night.

I sweep the meadow with the lantern, see that the sheep are huddled together on the hill, that the donkeys have gathered in the pole barn for the night.

Unlatching the gate, I walk over to the barn and slide the door open. Rose is alongside me at every step, her eyes sweeping along with the lantern light, taking in things I haven't begun to see or even suspect.

I look in on the chickens' roost to make sure no raccoons or other predators are lurking. On this particular December night, I spotted Winston and the two golden hens, but no Henrietta, which was slightly alarming.

"Heads up, Rose," I hissed, her signal to pay attention. Her ears went up and she tensed, then skittered off ahead, deeper into the barn. If something was amiss, Rose would let me know.

Meanwhile, where was Mother? She always greeted me when I entered the barn, balancing on the rafters, literally climbing the walls, purring and meowing for food and ear-scratching. Did Mother change her mind about tolerating

Henrietta? Did Henrietta wander off and meet a coyote or fox? Rose circled and sniffed as I moved farther into the darkened barn.

I heard purring and shone my lantern toward it.

Mother was curled on a pile of straw in the stall, eyes half closed, making sounds of contentment. Henrietta had perched right nearby on the wooden wall that separated the stalls, settled into the vegetative trance chickens enter at night.

Rose stared at this duo, but there was nothing to involve us further. Mother seemed pretty vegetative herself. I'd never seen behavior quite like this, but that was becoming par for the course.

I turned off the light, closed up the barn, and went to bed.

A FEW MORNINGS LATER, I went out to the barn. Rose usually heads like a rocket to the pasture gate, but this time she veered off sharply to the right, heading for the road. Something was wrong.

I walked to the edge of the driveway and froze. Henrietta was lying dead in the road. I could remember hearing a car speed by in the night, then hit its brakes, and I had wondered, sleepily, about it. Henrietta had almost surely dashed across the road and been hit.

She did dart across the road too quickly sometimes, unlike my other chickens, who seemed to know to stay away.

Rose came up to Henrietta and sniffed her, perhaps crossing the hen off her farm inventory list. Rose didn't waste time on sentiment.

I felt Henrietta; her body was already stiffening in the cold.

I picked her up and carried her back to the farmhouse door. I got a trash bag and put her body inside. Then I called Rose and I climbed onto the four-wheeler and ran out to the woods about half a mile.

Rose loped alongside. As always, she was present when an animal came to the farm, and present when one left.

She watched curiously as I stopped, walked out into the woods, and dumped Henrietta out of the bag, onto the ground.

I left her as a gift to the coyotes and the other woodland predators. I didn't wish to bury a chicken, nor hold a ceremony for her; it didn't seem appropriate.

"Goodbye, Henrietta," I said. "You were a pretty interesting chicken."

Chapter Four

MURDEROUS MOTHER

Ultimately, I fear, the question of whether
consciousness, forethought, reasoning, imagery and
rational planning exist in species other than our own
simply can't be answered conclusively until we have
gathered a lot more scientific data. What is more,
in animals, where language is not possible,
it is difficult even to know what evidence would be
sufficient to prove or disprove the existence of
consciousness and all its trappings.

—STANLEY COREN,
The Intelligence of Dogs

MOTHER, THE BARN CAT, MAY BE THE SINGLE MOST AF-
fectionate animal on Bedlam Farm, apart from the dogs.
Whenever I go into the barn or the pasture, she pops up, meowing and wrapping herself around my leg, or leaping onto
a convenient fencepost or stump so I can scratch her ears.

Mother often strolls along with me at night, darting

through the brush to keep up as I make my final rounds. Sometimes she even comes onto the front porch to yowl and draw me outside, where she takes possession of my lap while we stare out at the valley below, the farmhouses and barns bright pinpricks of light in the vast dark.

She's delighted when I pick her up and rub her head, which I do, faithfully. She's particularly delighted when I bring her special treats like a can of sardines.

She makes contact with me at no small risk. Rose has never fully accepted a cat's presence in her realm. Rose has had her nose raked and bloodied more than once by this tough little cat but won't acknowledge defeat. Mostly, the two of them maintain a wary truce.

Mother came to me as a young cat, a ratty wisp of a thing. A tortoiseshell with lovely black and white and ginger fur, she'd gotten her name because she watched out for everybody's kittens, not just her own. But the farmer who gave her to me had enough cats, and had no use for her. I did; my barns were overrun with rats and mice—what farm isn't?—and I didn't want to turn to pesticides.

I had Mother spayed, gave her the proper shots, and brought her a steady stream of kibble and canned food to help her fill out. It didn't seem to quell her desire to hunt, however. I don't have a rodent problem anymore.

I love Mother. She's my first cat, and she's taught me about the wildness cats retain, their indirect ways of loving, their intelligence, and their determination—unlike that of dogs—to live life on their own terms, not yours.

She has other fans, too. My friend Maria, the artist who works in my studio barn, is happy to have her company. Mother often materializes—especially on cold or stormy nights—and curls up in an old leather chair, purring for hours by the woodstove while Maria works.

Mother also adores Annie, following her around whether Annie is mucking out stalls or feeding sheep.

"Mother," Annie calls early every morning when she arrives and climbs out of her truck. Within seconds, the cat emerges from some crevice, tail up, meowing, and stays beside her, batting at dead leaves or baling wire to amuse herself. When Annie goes into the barn to move hay, Mother follows her, hopping from bale to bale.

The dairy barn is Mother's Palace; she rules with complete authority. She moves around the space like Spider-Man, hurtling straight up posts and across beams, diving behind hay bales, lazing way up in the rafters to soak up the late-afternoon sun. One wall, rising five feet from the floor, and thus safe from the vigilant Rose, is where Mother usually waits for me, purring and batting her enticing golden eyes. What a mysterious creature, I often think, so gentle and affectionate, yet so ferocious and undomesticated.

She has been a barn cat all her life—a tough job, marked by short life spans—and has never spent a night in a human dwelling. On the bitterest, snowiest nights, I invite her inside the farmhouse, but she never accepts.

Barn cats are mythic creatures hereabouts. They're hardy, and they have to be: Farmers can rarely pay for their immunizations or veterinary treatments. So barn cats fall prey to all kinds of trouble—they get felled by disease, hit by cars, attacked by predators, including people who shoot them for sport. Those fates, I'm determined, won't befall Mother. She does get medical treatment. She doesn't have to roam, because I feed her every day. And since she'll never come inside,

Annie has made a hay igloo for Mother that I wouldn't mind sleeping in, most nights.

Still, Mother is a barn cat. Every couple of months, she vanishes, for reasons I never know, and I worry that a coyote has gotten her, or that one of the pickups that zoom up and down the hilly road in front of my farm has hit her. After two or three days, she always returns. But one day, I suspect, she won't. That, too, is the lot of the barn cat.

HOWEVER LOVINGLY Mother greets me, she's also the most deadly creature I've ever known.

Mother is all about mayhem and violence. When she isn't cuddling with one of her many human friends and admirers, she is killing things. She kills mice and rats, of course, but also birds—any kind she can. She kills moles and chipmunks and eviscerates frogs, toads, and snakes.

When I come outside each morning, I find dismembered animals, or parts thereof, left as gifts for me: rodent limbs, birds' heads and wings, unidentifiable organs.

I frequently look out my study window to see Mother stalking or playing with a corpse, tossing mice or birds in the air and catching them, batting them around. Most of my farm animals are placid vegetarians. Not this one.

UNTIL I HAD BACK TROUBLE one winter, I'd been caring for the swelling population of Bedlam Farm largely by myself, hauling hay and water, tending to hooves, dispensing grain and feed.

Even after treatment helped relieve my pain, I knew I couldn't handle all the chores any longer. Square bales of hay look light, but they weigh fifty pounds each. I sometimes lean more heavily than I used to on my walking sticks.

I hired Annie to haul the hay and grain buckets around on weekdays. Maria, a restorer of old buildings as well as an artist, helps out on weekends in exchange for the use of the studio barn.

So I was looking forward to Christmas, an unseasonably warm day, when Annie would be off duty and Maria away, and I was once again alone with my animal charges. My only plans were to bring some friends their Christmas presents, then hang around the farm and read by the kindly woodstoves, walk with the dogs. It was a bittersweet holiday; my wife, Paula, and I had separated earlier in the year. Emma, my daughter, was covering a New York Giants game and would arrive in a few days with Pearl, the sweet-tempered yellow Lab she'd borrowed (with no real intent to return her) for fledgling-writer support.

So Christmas was very quiet—no phone calls, no visitors, no plans. It was a good day to hang around with the sheep and donkeys, cows and chickens, species that were some of the original participants in that long-ago manger scene (well, except for the chickens).

I got up early, took Rose and Izzy out to the barn. Rose's role is to hold the hungry sheep at bay while I drag out the hay and fill the feeders. Izzy, still useless when it comes to farm tasks, merely lies down and looks appealing. I spent a long time watching Mother, who jumped onto my shoulder, purred as I stroked her, then headed off to slay something.

This is what Aristotle and Aquinas were trying to get at, in the harsher, more limited contexts of their own times. This is what they were trying to say. As I watched Mother, things grew clearer.

Mother is not loving or good, I thought. Nor is she evil. She's the embodiment of animal instincts, not of the sensitive rational soul Aristotle goes on and on about. She represents the very thing so many people don't want to believe about their pets—that they don't think like us, don't choose us consciously or rationally, are not able to make moral decisions, and so can't be held responsible for what they do. In certain central respects, in fact, Mother is the antithesis of what people mean by souls.

If dogs and cats are like us, think like us, have souls like ours, then Mother is the Khmer Rouge, a brutal killer who massacres indiscriminately. She's no sweet soul bound for heaven.

But I suspect that, instead, she's a remarkable animal, bristling with instinct, acting out genetically encoded impulses while keeping my farm remarkably free of rats. She's amazing, admirable.

I love the birds that visit the feeder hung outside my study window. Blue jays, woodpeckers, chickadees, sparrows, swallows, cardinals, robins—one or two have even landed briefly on my outstretched arm or shoulder on occasion. They fill the day with song and color and beauty.

It's not easy to sit at my desk day after day and watch them get slaughtered, especially when my own feeders are helping to lure them to their deaths. Mother, it turns out, hides behind the garbage cans below the feeders and when her prey come for sunflower seeds and suet, she pounces. I moved the trash cans, but Mother merely found another hiding place behind the adjacent stone wall. I've raised and moved the feeders, but wherever they are, seed spills out onto the ground, birds swoop down on it, and Mother routinely picks them off, one after another.

Mother doesn't just murder; she seems to enjoy prolonging her victims' suffering. She maims before she kills. Drawn by awful screams, I caught her torturing baby rabbits one af-

ternoon in the big barn across the street, and briefly wanted
to kick her. I caught myself, of course, reminding myself it
was just her instinct, her genes being true to her history.

Watching her stalk a field mouse on Christmas Day, I re-
flected that while our dogs and cats have grown ever more
domesticated, while we've become affluent, needy, or perhaps generous enough to treat them extraordinarily well,
Aristotle's argument has held up.

If Mother were equal to or superior to humans in her self-
awareness, consciousness, soul, and spirit; if she were, as so
many people say of their pets, "just like a child," then probably
I should call the police, have Mother arrested or committed.

For that matter, if that were really my view—that she was
a sentient, self-conscious, self-aware, and moral being—
shouldn't I punish her severely, or even kill her myself?

Mother wasn't killing in self-defense or for food. She had
ample nourishment without these victims. Yet in just a day
she'd slaughter two or three or more small, defenseless creatures, simply because it was her nature. And while nobody,
surely not I, knows what goes on inside an animal's head, she
sure seemed to be having a good time doing it, batting her
victims around like Ping-Pong balls.

I'm working to gain some perspective on this conundrum.
This killing is, I know, natural for cats. I love Mother anyway,
and she shows great affection for me. I not only cherish her,
I depend on the very brutality that sometimes startles me. She
has vanquished the rats that invaded my farm and barns, steal-
ing food, possibly spreading disease and menacing the other
animals. She keeps the mice at bay. An exceptional animal,
she teaches me much.

But when notions of good and evil get kicked around,
Mother reminds me not to apply them to animals. What

Aristotle argues—that the most precious aspect of the human soul is the ability to reason and make choices, and that since animals can't do that, they can't be compared to us—is so true of Mother that it shocks me. It doesn't mean she is inferior to me, but it bracingly reminds me how different she is. Human-like notions of good or bad can't be applied to her and, for both her sake and ours, they ought not be. We're responsible for the choices we make; she isn't.

Think how many cats, dogs, and other pets suffer from being measured against human notions of good behavior, of how many animals get beaten, abused, even killed, because we judge them by human terms.

IN THE MOST IRONIC of situations, therefore, I was bringing a Christmas gift to my bizarrely contradictory barn cat, offering her a can of yummy, oily sardines while looking warily around the barn floor for any fresh kills.

"Mother," I said, "you are a butcher, an indiscriminate slaughterer of living things that pose no threat, give no food or sustenance, mean you no harm. How can you be so loving to me?"

She meowed in her squeaky way, hopped flirtatiously up onto her favorite post, and—keeping an eye out for Rose—leaped into my arms, purring constantly. We cuddled for a few minutes, our reverie interrupted by bellowing from Elvis, who'd heard my voice and was awaiting his own snack.

"Can't keep Elvis waiting," I told Mother, giving her the last of the sardines. If he got annoyed, he could probably stroll right through the (closed) barn door. Mother hopped down, to accompany me on the rest of my rounds. She was a friend of my cow and steers.

A few minutes later, back in the house, I was watching the songbirds flitting about the feeder. I saw Mother's agile form slink across the driveway and disappear behind the trunk of the tree from which the feeder hung. I banged on the window and yelled, which prompted Rose to bark, and the birds took off. Mother, looking betrayed, trotted back to the barn, but they'd be back, and so would she.

Don't I owe them protection? Shouldn't Mother be stopped, somehow? I could probably find other ways to get rid of rats. But living on a farm is a model for dealing with nature and its simple, unwavering, and sometimes lethal realities. There are no animal rights on a farm, really, only the intricate, intertwined web of species, instinct, and survival.

Every day, the birds and mice and rats still come. They don't understand what awaits them, nor do the experiences of their peers seem to alter their behavior. They—and Mother—act out their timeless rituals. Minutes after a bird is dismembered outside my window, a score more will appear to dine, their lost comrade in full view.

If animals lack human-style consciousness, if they act purely out of instinct, why do we have so much trouble accepting that? Why do we need so badly to remake them in our own image?

In earlier ages, people generally agreed that animals had been placed in the world to be at man's disposal. Genesis taught that man had been given dominion over nature, just as Aristotle insisted that "nature has made all the animals for the sake of men." Human superiority, he wrote, lay in the fact that while plants possessed a "vegetative" soul and animals a "sensitive" soul, humans alone could boast a rational soul.

Today, such notions sound arrogant, outdated. In an ongoing reassessment, animals have become romanticized, emotionalized, humanized. In fact, one hears all the time that animals are our superiors—simpler, more honest, loving, dependable. We've been demoted, while they're increasingly considered to have, and deserve, rights, protections, legal status—and, possibly, an afterlife.

Consider this Milan Kundera poem, meant to express how much our animals mean to us, but also illustrating how rapidly humans have lost ground since Tudor times:

> Dogs are our link to paradise.
> They don't know evil or jealousy or discontent.
> With a dog on a hillside on a glorious afternoon is to be back in
>   Eden,
> where doing nothing was not boring—it was peace.

The curious thing about that poem is that I've not only read it, but felt it. A couple of days before Christmas, in this lovely but freakishly warm winter, Rose and I took the sheep across the road to the meadow. It was sunny, the grass still green, and I was awash in wonderful dogs.

Rose was overseeing the sheep down in the meadow, keeping them in line. Izzy had flopped down next to me, lying on his back, awaiting belly scratches.

Mother appeared behind us, popping out of the tall grass as she often does when we are herding—I can't imagine how she moves so quickly and covers so much ground with such stealth. Sizing up where Rose was, she tiptoed up behind me, purring, and flopped onto her back, too.

To me, these animals *were* a link to paradise, and I *was* back in Eden, far from the ugly headlines of the day. Mother, like the dogs, did not know "evil or jealousy or discontent." Nor did she know that she had no reason any longer to kill and torture birds and rabbits.

Watching her, meeting her eyes, responding to her demand for attention, I could see why this argument was so important to people trying to make sense of the world. Good people were supposed to be rewarded, bad people punished, and reason was the means by which they made their choices. If animals lacked that capacity, how could they be punished or rewarded in this or any world? Why should they bother to be good or bad, as we are constantly training and imploring them to be?

Liberal-minded contemporary theologians grasp that many of the old, cruel views of animals need updating. We've learned that some animals are more involved and intelligent than Aristotle could possibly have known. And many of us have also come to see the human race as less entitled to its dominion, since we're making such a rotten job of it.

Walking around, visiting with my animals on Christmas— after I brought Elvis his candy bar, fed the donkeys and sheep stale bread and apples, and treated the dogs to basted bones— I felt grateful to be able to walk among these sweet and simple creatures, and to learn from them. A life in Boston or Philadelphia, New York City or suburban New Jersey—all places I have lived—no longer felt possible, mostly because *they* couldn't be there with me.

So, certain philosophers and theologians strike a chord with me when they challenge us to include animals in our notions of mercy and love, to pay greater attention to them as sentient beings. The question, really, is how far to take those arguments, and how much of the earlier ones to keep.

Watching Mother later that Christmas afternoon as she

stalked yet another bird, I did wonder—for her sake—if we weren't doing animals a disservice by believing they had our style of souls, perhaps misunderstanding them in the process, even putting them at risk.

Mother traveled low to the ground, silently, bloodily effective at what she did. There was no way, I thought, that I was looking at a good creature, or a bad one. Only at one that I respected and loved, and that, in some indefinable way, seemed to love me back.

And that was good enough.

Chapter Five

BRUTUS AND LENORE

I think we turn so much to our pets because they
remind us of our deeper nature, of what is truly
important. And also in a strange way of what we can
be. They rest us deeply and give us sudden joys
that we have forgotten.

—Jean Houston

THE SPRING HAD BEGUN WITH A LONG DRY SPELL. THEN,
even after the rains came, the main pasture behind the
farmhouse didn't spring into its usual lush greenness. It pro-
duced more weeds than grass, which would have made a fine
diet for goats, but wouldn't sustain my hungry sheep.

I recognized, with chagrin, that I'd allowed this field to
become overgrazed, that I should have reseeded it. I would
arrange that next spring, but now, either I had to order many
more bales of hay to feed the sheep for some weeks—an expensive solution—or I had to take them into the farther
meadows to graze each day.

Accordingly, Rose and I began each morning—early, before the sun got too strong—by herding the flock through the gate and escorting them to literally greener pastures.

Sometimes we went up the hill, sometimes across the road. Then we sat and kept vigil for an hour or so while the sheep crunched happily at the abundant grass, and later escorted them back, repeating the procedure in early evening. It was a hot, buggy, and time-consuming routine, though not without its quiet pleasures.

Rose, of course, was delighted to have additional opportunities to boss her flock around. She kept a judicious eye on the sheep at all times. Since she did, I was free to listen to music on my iPod, read a book, mull on the larger meaning of life. Lenore was also a good muller, though of little use as a herder, so I took to bringing her along for company.

At first she was anxious, staying back, even hiding in the tall grass when the sheep approached. Then, day by day, she became bolder, more curious.

I was sitting on a rock and reading one morning when, in my peripheral vision, I noticed Lenore sidling over toward the grazing Brutus, one of my wethers (neutered rams). I dropped my book and sprinted over. Sheep don't like dogs much. Even Rose has been kicked, butted, and charged at, especially by rams, who are notoriously grumpy.

Lenore, just eleven months old, had in her young life encountered few animals or people that didn't respond to her genial nature. She didn't seem to grasp the idea of inherent hostility, either in humanity or in the animal world.

Labs are famously affectionate and outgoing, but Lenore had an especially charismatic personality, even by Labrador standards. I got her when I was in the midst of a gripping depression; I needed a love dog, and she obliged. I suspect I reinforced her tendency toward affection. It had been bred into her, but it also developed and was strengthened by my relationship with her, my work with her.

It showed, not only with me and with other people but, curiously enough, with the other animals on the farm. Lenore began courting the no-nonsense Rose, who rarely deigned to play, and Izzy, who was focused on people and didn't seem to care much about other dogs. She greeted Mother, the barn cat, who ran from her at first, then drew closer. She went nose-to-nose with the goats and the donkeys through the pasture fence; she seemed eager to befriend every animal on the place.

I expected that Brutus would run, or perhaps butt her. My own attitude toward sheep is mixed: I like and care for them, but they always seem too uniform to be interesting, with their elemental concern about food and rest and not much else. Besides, I'm almost never near a sheep without a border collie next to me; sheep are unlikely to find that endearing.

But Lenore was focusing on Brutus, and he wasn't running away. He stared at her, somewhat exasperated, as if assuming he was going to have to move, but Lenore dropped to the ground, a submissive position. Brutus looked at her for a long while, then lowered his head.

Uh-oh. I was close now, about ten feet away, ready to rescue Lenore, when she reached up and, astonishingly, licked Brutus's nose. And he let her.

It was the beginning of one of those interspecies animal friendships you see in movies but rarely in life. In fact, I'm often struck by how closely species stick together. The cows are always within a few feet of each other; the donkeys are inseparable; and I've never seen the sheep show much curiosity about creatures without fleece.

Either Lenore's charms were especially persuasive, or Brutus was a very strange sheep. Or both.

Brutus had been born on this farm, pulled out of his mother by me on a brutally cold morning the first winter we had lambs. He's easy with people, mostly even-tempered, though it's not unheard of for him to charge or butt another sheep—or even me, if I'm not looking. Rose has tangled with him several times—she brooks no rebellion from sheep—so he's generally well behaved.

Still, the sight of Brutus and Lenore meeting in the meadow was striking. I laughed out loud, and reached for my camera.

I didn't see that any good could come from this relationship. He isn't good for you, I told Lenore, adopting a protective paternalism. The other sheep will turn on you. Rose will never accept it. This can't go anywhere.

Rose, in fact, was already staring incredulously as Lenore curled up next to Brutus, gave him another lick, and took a nap while he grazed a few feet away.

But the ritual continued over the next couple of weeks. The two would find each other, bump noses. Brutus lowered his head for a slurp, then grazed while Lenore sat or lay beside him.

Once in a while, another sheep—especially Brutus's mother, Paula—drifted over to try to figure out what was going on.

Rose did seem to have a rough time of it. This fraternization undermined the sense of order she always strove to maintain. Sheep did what they were told, period, and dogs didn't commune with them, linger with them in a far corner of the pasture, or lick them on the nose. That wasn't the way Rose worked.

Here, I thought, were the souls of two dogs colliding. Lenore loved every creature she met. Rose lived for work.

Yet the two of them seemed to work it out over the next few weeks. Rose got nervous whenever Lenore and Brutus drifted too far from the rest of the sheep and would go fetch Brutus, making him return to the flock, without Lenore. So they learned to stay closer to the flock.

Lenore made a few other friends, too—another ram, a couple of ewes—but Brutus remained her main squeeze. After a while, he automatically lowered his head when she approached, presenting his nose and ear for licking.

Eventually, Rose came to accept this odd couple in her midst, and either worked around them or simply ignored them. Lenore, after she'd visited awhile with Brutus, would come over to lie by Rose—another transgression. Rose hadn't permitted Lenore near her when she was working, as if she sensed that this less disciplined creature would bring chaos.

But now, Rose seemed to enjoy it, and the sight of these two beautiful working dogs, each faithful to her own nature, was touching, even calming.

I loved, too, that all this had happened with no involvement by me, beyond my experience, commands, or control. All sorts of things were going on in the pasture daily— between Lenore and Brutus, Rose and the sheep, Rose and Lenore, the dogs and me. Some of it I was aware of, some of it I wasn't; I had no clear idea of what anybody was up to, or why.

The best theory I could come up with was that Lenore had been rewarded for her loving nature from puppyhood. I needed it at the time, I reveled in it, and beamed when she approached people or other animals in her joyous, enthusiastic way. Rose has no such agenda.

Each dog responds to what's innate in them, and also to what I ask of them. Rose works for me and Lenore loves me. That's where our souls converge.

IT WAS A HOT, sticky July afternoon. A haze had settled over the valley, and the farm was very still. My dogs lay in the shade near the garden.

Suddenly, I heard them bark. A car had overheated on the road right in front of my farmhouse. A young couple emerged, the guy fiddling under the hood, muttering, and the mother comforting two fussing girls.

It was oppressively humid. The black flies that torture my animals were swarming everywhere, as they do around farms in summer. The kids—one seemed about three or four, the other perhaps six—looked and sounded miserable.

I went and asked if anybody needed help, but the young parents seemed shy, anxious not to disturb. The father, hard at work under the hood, had the air of somebody who didn't like asking for help.

The border collies, Izzy and Rose, were still barking through the fence; Lenore had her paws up on the fence, her tail wagging furiously. I got some bottled water out of the refrigerator, called Lenore, and walked back down the driveway. "Can I bring you some water?" I called.

The father, peering out from under the hood, nodded. The mother looked apprehensively to her girls, who had stopped whimpering and were staring at Lenore, making a beeline down the driveway, her tail going a mile a minute.

"They aren't really used to dogs," the woman said hesitantly, eyeing this big black dog trotting toward them. But I said that Lenore was very gentle and loved children, and was it okay to bring her over? The mother said, well, okay, and waved us across.

Lenore wiggled over to the girls—Chrissy and Katie, we learned. At first, the girls backed away, fascinated but wary. Then Lenore plopped down next to them and rolled over on her back, exuding so much unthreatening pleasure that, almost instantly, both girls were on their knees on either side of her, laughing and squealing and leaning over for Lenore's licks. She sat up and happily accepted more pats and hugs.

Lenore radiated affection, but she also seemed to know, instinctively, not to jump on the little girls or knock them over, not to overwhelm them. This, it struck me, was also a dog at work, a dog with boundless heart whose instincts led her to share it.

Watching her work, I saw her joy spread through this harried family. The two girls were leaning over her to hug her; the father looked out from under the hood and laughed. "We need to get the girls a dog," he said. The young mother, hot and weary, was smiling, joining in the Lenore lovefest.

Lenore presented herself appropriately to the children, charmed the mother, and when she was done with that, came around the car to lick the father's shoe and wiggle her tail at him. When I went back into the house, all four were laughing, joking, drinking their water, talking about getting a puppy. "Goodbye, Lenore!" I heard the kids shout from the road.

———

SHE CERTAINLY HADN'T consciously decided to do what she'd done. To some extent, she didn't have to: Lenore is well bred, of a good-tempered lineage; she was already inclined to like people and be sociable.

I've bolstered this behavior, no doubt, by continually taking her to stores, friends' houses, book events, hospice visits, bringing her into unfamiliar situations, giving her the opportunity to meet all kinds of people. I've made it clear to her that affection is welcomed, and she gets praise for it, further helping to develop a natural trait.

It can seem like a tiny thing, walking across the road to amuse some children, yet to me, it was a big thing. The power to bring smiles to four uncomfortable and anxious people, to introduce children to the pleasure of a canine companion, to promote the love of animals—none of those was a small thing.

And Lenore did it all the time, multiplied the impact of that little visit by hundreds of encounters with hundreds of people. She went with me to a local high school and helped nervous students in a writing course I taught relax and feel easier with me, with one another. She goes into one hospice home after another, sad places sometimes, where suddenly there is a bit of laughter. Here and there, in this interaction and that, fifty times a day, she turns on the lights.

If there's magic in the relationships between humans and dogs, it might be that mysterious interdependence, the ways in which we sometimes need our dogs greatly, and some of them can read that and become the dogs we need. In this way, they steady us, buoy us, especially in dark times.

This love, the impact it has on human beings, is Lenore's work. Whether it will get her into heaven or not rests in much more knowing hands than mine. It's not really a question someone like me can answer.

But I can see why so many people find almost ludicrous the idea that dogs lack souls and might therefore be barred from the afterlife. God made them, after all. God loves us, and we love dogs. The scene on my road this summer day shows one reason why.

One summer night, not long after that, when I was tired and my back hurt and I was feeling discouraged, I crawled into bed early, with a good book. I took a deep breath and tried to settled myself. It had been a rough day.

I knew that in a minute or two, though, I would hear a clacking and a panting as Lenore barreled up the stairs, and I was right. A black shadow entered the bedroom. Her big, smooth, squarish head appeared by the bedside; I could feel a breeze from the wagging tail.

I bent over and leaned my forehead against hers. "Hey, Love Hound," I said, and she slurped at my face. Then she hopped up, curled herself into a ball, and nestled herself against my ribs.

I smiled.

Chapter Six

THE SOUL OF ROSE

The gate opens   I'm good at this
my heart awaits, limbs taut   crouch and wait
I hear Jon's command   give them time
"get the sheep"   round in back
hugging the meadow   down the hill
knowing my mission   through the gate
there you are sheep   now settle you sheep
I will make you move   I'll lie and watch

—MARY KELLOGG

I HAD A FEW FRIENDS OVER FOR DINNER ONE NEW YEAR'S Eve. Among the guests was Maria the artist. Apart from Annie and me, Maria may be the only human Rose loves.

This makes a certain amount of sense. Like Rose, Maria has a ferocious work ethic. It's as common to see her up on ladders in broiling heat or brutal cold, restoring old buildings to service and beauty, as it is to see Rose moving the sheep in mud, ice, or midsummer sun. Like Rose, Maria is loving and loyal, with a sense of vulnerability, a self one can never see completely.

Normally, when Rose is working, humans barely exist. Even when she's not herding, people aren't of much interest. She doesn't charm, the way Izzy and Lenore do; she's rarely in anyone's lap. When she sees Maria, though, she comes running over, full of tail wags and kisses, almost Lab-like.

On this holiday eve, though, Rose hopped up onto the couch next to Maria despite all the other guests nearby. She showed Maria her belly. "What's wrong, Rose?" Maria asked, stroking her. I mentioned that Rose hadn't been eating much for a day or two—probably she'd ingested some decaying thing. Rose licked Maria's hand.

It startled me, and Maria as well, this submissive posture. It's rare for Rose to appear at all when there's company, uncharacteristic. Rose doesn't care for New Year's Eve celebrations any more than I do. Something unusual was passing between these two.

Maria felt it, too. Rose was sending someone she loved and trusted a message of some sort, perhaps one I'd been slow to pick up on: She needed help.

Rose had been herding as usual, but afterward, she'd been sluggish. Her appetite, never hearty, was off. I'd been thinking of taking her to see our vet.

After a few moments, as people drifted into the living room, Rose left the couch, walked into my office, and crawled beneath the printer, one of her favorite spots. I didn't see her again until everyone had left. But I knew we'd be at the vet's on January 2.

ROSE POSES A PERENNIAL CHALLENGE when it comes to health care. She's been kicked by donkeys, butted by rams. She's torn her paws in rocky pastures and on tangles of old wire in the woods. She once ran underneath the tires of the ATV. Her folder at the vet's is fattening to telephone-book dimensions.

She's lucky to be alive, and I am luckier still.

Often, she'll scarf down some dubious food when her prey drive is high—donkey or sheep manure, maybe part of a dead animal carcass. A day or two of vomiting generally follows, after which her digestive system recovers.

You hardly ever know, if you're not paying strict attention, when Rose is truly sick. The vet calls her stoic; I'd say she's astonishingly indifferent to pain. Once, while she was herding sheep, I noticed a slight limp (her right leg was broken). Another time, she lay on the bed next to me, and only when she got up did I notice bloodstains on the sheets (she'd impaled herself on a stone or possibly a shard of glass, the vet said).

I often fear that Rose won't live to reach old age, and that's troubling for many reasons: I love her, but I also doubt that I could keep this farm functioning without her.

Probably I could keep her safer by confining her more, but that's not the life Rose is destined for, it seems to me. She's a working farm dog, from a proud tradition; she needs—deserves—to be free to do her job, watch the sheep, cover my back.

I do take precautions. Rose never goes outside alone, out of my sight. I've fenced several areas around the farmhouse, so that she can hang out and observe her sheep when I'm busy or away. But she's never left to run unsupervised. Still, she manages to injure herself with some frequency.

ON NEW YEAR'S DAY, Rose was up and ready to run as always. Whatever had been bothering her the night before seemed to have eased.

When I feed the dogs in the morning, Rose keeps an eye on the mudroom, where I leave my shoes. If I put on sneakers, she'll eat her kibble. If I choose rubber pasture boots, she knows we are going out to the sheep. In that case, I put her bowl on the counter for later, knowing she won't bother with breakfast until her herding's done. Given the choice, Rose would much rather work than eat.

This day I pulled on my rubber boots because rain had rendered the countryside a boggy mess. So I had no opportunity to gauge Rose's appetite.

We—Rose, Izzy, and I—were about to usher in the new year with one of our favorite things: an ATV ride through the woods, border collie nirvana.

I crank up the ATV and putt-putt down the driveway.

When I reach the dirt road in front of the farm, I hold up my arm and yell, "Stay!" Rose and Izzy go into their best border collie crouches and freeze. When I've checked the road for traffic, I look over my shoulder. Izzy is usually about ten feet off on my left, Rose poised up on the hill behind me, both tensed for action.

If all is clear, I yell, "Go!" and the two dogs shoot ahead like bullets from a rifle, catapulting down the dirt path across the road, into the woods. I motor after them, but I can never quite keep pace.

Every quarter of a mile or so, they spin around and crouch, facing me, waiting until I'm just a couple of hundred feet away. Then they turn and sprint off again. When I catch up to them a mile or so up the path, both are lying in a clearing, waiting for me, their tongues long. In warm weather, I bring a jug of water and a collapsible bowl. I turn off the ATV and sit on a tree trunk, offer a drink.

I may have brought a book to read, or the three of us may

just stare out into the woods, collecting ourselves. Izzy will eventually sniff about a bit. But however speedily Rose has been running, she doesn't move as long as I'm sitting with her, reading or thinking.

After fifteen minutes or half an hour, by which time the dogs are no longer even breathing heavily, I start up the ATV and Rose takes off ahead of me. I've never passed her.

Few dogs are as well adapted to sheer joyful running as border collies, who can travel long distances at high speeds without damaging their joints or limbs the way Labs might. It helps calm and settle them.

It isn't the only exercise Rose gets, but she especially loves flat-out running, and it's done her good. Jeff Meyer, the vet, says she has one of the strongest heartbeats he's heard in a dog, and that she's remarkably healthy and fit. (So is Izzy, though he doesn't go quite as far or as fast.)

It helps her with herding, too. Even when the flock takes off, Rose easily outflanks the sheep, heads them off, turns them around. If they're balking, she can scamper up and down hills all day, rarely tiring or even slowing.

On New Year's, after our morning outing, I put the ATV in the barn, walked with Izzy and Rose back into the house, and put her untouched food bowl on the floor. No dice. She wouldn't even give breakfast a sniff.

Then she followed me into my office and put her head on my knee, another unusual gesture. So whatever had been bothering her hadn't resolved itself. I got onto the floor and cradled her in my arms. "What's the matter, sweetie?" I asked. She vomited.

JEFF SHOWED ME THE X-RAY. Something had lodged in her stomach, blocking food, and our ATV run might have caused further damage. I felt stricken as he gestured at the squarish object at the bottom of her stomach; even I could see that it shouldn't be there. Jeff couldn't identify what it was, but he needed to find out and scheduled surgery for the next morning. Meanwhile, Rose had to stay at his clinic; she'd become dehydrated and needed intravenous fluids.

At home, I tended to farm chores, took the other dogs for a walk, tried to work. Izzy kept looking around for Rose. I'd planned to move the sheep, so that Annie could bring the grain out unmolested, but I couldn't. All of us were off balance without Rose.

I called the vet's office to see if I could come visit Rose in the evening, before her surgery. Sure, the tech said, come on by. I brought Izzy along, and the two of us threaded through the back rooms to the presurgical area. Rose, lying in a large crate with an IV tube taped to one foreleg, was happy to see us, wriggling and sticking her nose through the crate's bars to lick me. I reached my fingers through to scratch her nose.

"Hang in there," I told her. "And get your ass back on the farm. The sheep will run amok, the donkeys will misbehave, and I ain't living there without you, period." We sat with her for a few minutes.

I talked with Jeff, then with the techs, who sounded reassuring. But back out in the parking lot with Izzy, my eyes filled with tears.

At such times, dogs seem to act like spigots, opening up hidden parts of ourselves. Jeff was a great vet and had performed such surgery many times. Rose was probably not in real peril.

I was frightened and sorrowful. We'd been through so much together; she'd been so true to me. I hoped our ATV romp hadn't made her condition more dangerous.

Sitting on the concrete steps in the parking lot, I wiped my eyes. Izzy sat behind me, waiting and silent.

Two day later, she was home, back at work.

THE SUMMER BEFORE, an enormous crew of people had descended on Washington County to shoot a movie of one of my earlier books, *A Dog Year*. Producers, actors, caterers, grips, drivers, production assistants—they were everywhere.

In my barn, residents for several weeks, were five border collies, assembled from Hollywood and other points around the country, who would play Orson. Every morning after they were fed and exercised, they were made up—complete with tinted contact lenses, hair extensions, and fur coloring—so they'd all look alike. They were gorgeous dogs, cute and perky and well trained; they tolerated such cosmetic fussing the way any star would. They weren't, in other words, like my dogs. Rose, in particular, seemed disgruntled by their presence in her barn.

On almost the same day the movie people arrived, as if by some secret signal, my ewes began lambing. By my calculations, the lambs weren't due for two months, but I'd been off before. The first time I bred the sheep, the lambs were born in February, in the midst of the worst winter in decades. This time, blessedly, it was summer, so weather was not a factor; no lambs were in danger of dying from the cold.

Still, chaos threatened. Once I saw what was happening, and told the movie crew, they graciously insisted on building a temporary lambing pen inside the dog fence behind the house. A few sheets of plywood nailed together was what I had in mind, but that wasn't substantial enough for the film carpenters. Big white trucks began depositing wood, tin roofing, and other supplies, and construction started. But the carpenters were pulled off the job to work on sets, and the lambs had already begun dropping.

We went into emergency lambing mode. Annie and I hauled out syringes, towels, tail-dockers, medicines, and milk supplements. Rose went from alert to hypervigilant.

When I saw two or three ewes still circling and straining one late afternoon, I knew we were headed for an all-nighter. I brought out biscuits and granola bars, bottled water and dog food, and set up a little encampment next to what we'd started calling the HBO Memorial Lambing Pen—so far, still a depression in the ground and a pile of plywood. I erected some temporary fencing under the apple tree; on a warm night, the lambs and ewes would be fine there.

After sunset, as the ewes were still doing their Lamaze breathing, Rose and I settled on a blanket with a powerful electrical torch and a cell phone (to call for reinforcements) and waited, Rose's eyes fixed on the mothers-to-be. She and Annie and I had painstakingly collected the pregnant ewes, the humans grabbing them with hands and crooks as Rose pushed the flock through the gate, so we were now in the dog run with about a dozen sheep, the rest nestled at the top of the pasture.

We watched as ewe Number 96 (only two or three of the sheep had names) began more active labor, lying on her side, her head upraised, straining visibly. She had a long and difficult labor, groaning and bleating for two hours. There was little we midwives could do to help but wait and watch. I brought 96 a bucket of water, which she gulped eagerly.

This was taking too long. One of my biggest and oldest ewes, she was growing exhausted, and I worried that her lamb might be in trouble. I moved behind her and looked beneath her tail. She tried to bolt, but Rose kept her in place.

I thought I saw the lamb's large head beginning to appear, though the area around it was swollen and dry. But it was hard to see clearly in the darkness, and I couldn't hold the ewe completely still for a good look. Should I call the large-animal vet? But I'd seen in previous years that the vets often couldn't do much more than I could; besides, I'd learned a lot from them, namely how to reach in and properly position a lamb's head and legs, and then pull.

The ewe, too weary to remain standing, lay down to rest. So did I, Rose beside me. But her eyes stayed locked on 96.

Sometime later, I woke up. Rose was sitting across from the ewe, who was on her feet again. Suddenly, as she gave a grunt, her water broke. At this point, if I'd had a lambing pen, the ewe would have been in it, rather than in this large fenced dog run.

Now time became critical. Within a half hour or so after the water breaks a lamb can die, and so can the ewe. "Rose, get the sheep," I said quietly. She had an uncanny ability to grasp a task; having been raised as a farm dog, rather than trained for herding trials, she almost always seemed to intuit what I needed. She'd been focusing on this ewe—ignoring the others on the far side of the run—all night.

Rose followed my command, staying in front of the ewe and backing her slowly toward me. I saw the lamb's head beginning to emerge, gray and cold, the eyes closed and swollen. I called Annie on my cell; she said she'd be right over.

The ewe suddenly scrambled away, but Rose circled ahead of her. I got a crook around her neck and wrestled her onto her side, quietly asking her forgiveness for the rough treatment. In a few minutes Annie came zooming into the driveway in her truck.

I wasn't able to hold the ewe at that point, my back complaining loudly; she struggled to her feet and took off. Rose cornered her, though, at the long end of the run. Annie came rushing up and, with Rose's help, we took up positions on either side of the ewe, and I grabbed her by the shoulders. We rolled her onto her side. She was too tired to put up much of a fight at this point. Rose backed away and watched.

As Annie held the ewe's head and shoulders, I got behind her with the torch. The lamb's head was protruding, but it felt lifeless. Clearly the lamb had gotten stuck in the birth canal. I regretted having waited so long to call Annie. Still, the lamb had to come out, or we'd lose the mother, too.

I reached inside and slid my right hand under the head, feeling for the legs to make sure they were pushed back. There was still fluid inside; it felt warm. I moved my hand behind the lamb's feet and then, with my other hand, got a grip on its jaw and pulled as hard as I could, the ewe moaning, and Annie pulling in the opposite direction.

I was almost too tired to move; I could only imagine what the poor ewe was feeling. Suddenly, the lamb's body came sliding out and I fell backward onto the grass with it. It lay unmoving and cold, eyes shut.

The first casualty of the lambing season, I remarked to Annie. She looked stricken, but pointed out that at least the mother was alive. We tended to her, bringing her some hay and fresh water laced with molasses, for energy. For some minutes she lay perfectly still, resting.

Suddenly, Annie's eyes widened; she pointed over my shoulder. "Look!" The lamb's chest was heaving, and Rose was licking at its wet body.

We rushed over to towel the baby's face; it opened both its

eyes and began to struggle to its feet. We brought it quickly to Number 96, who recognized it instantly and began to clear its eyes and mouth, nosing it to stand up. In a few minutes, we'd nudged the pair into the fenced area beneath the apple tree. The lamb was nursing, the ewe sipping her molasses water. If mother and baby couldn't occupy the HBO Memorial Lambing Pen, at least they could be snuggled together, apart from the rest of the maternity ward. Annie made them a bed of straw.

Three more lambs were born that night, the other births uneventful and by-the-numbers: a set of twins and another female. Annie headed back to bed. All Rose and I had to do was watch, wait for the licking and nuzzling, and administer vitamins and other shots.

It was a happy and successful night, but also filthy, grinding, and chilly. I fell asleep leaning against the pasture fence, Rose curled up a few feet away.

I was awakened by her low growling and felt something licking at the back of my head. The movie-star dogs, out for their morning stroll, had come over to the dog run and were sitting in a row, eyes wide, ears up. Cute and clean, they looked like curious spectators at a sporting event. Rose and I, on the other hand, were covered in manure, amniotic fluid, blood, and milk, and were surrounded by all sorts of debris. Towels, syringes, and bottles were strewn about.

"Morning, guys," I said to the perky onlookers. But something seemed to snap in Rose. She wriggled through a gap below the fence, went straight at the movie dogs, and chased them back into the barn, where they would soon be picked up and ferried to the set, ready for their close-ups.

This was not like Rose, who ignored almost all other

dogs, especially if she was working. But who says dogs lack self-awareness? Maybe she couldn't stand that they were so clean.

THOMAS AQUINAS SHAPED THE LIVES of many generations of animals when he wrote that irrational creatures like animals are not "god-possessors" and, thus, not fitting beneficiaries of good deeds. They cannot be equated with us, in his view—or mistreated.

When I went to visit Rose in the veterinary hospital, I was expressing concern for her, worrying about her—things she couldn't do for herself and couldn't do for me. In mainstream Christian theology, Rose had no status as a moral being. She could not possess the cornerstone element of a soul: the ability to make moral choices.

Rose's guidance through this tricky night, one of many, and her pardonable annoyance with the movie stars—great dogs all, and working dogs themselves—highlighted again just how remarkable she is. But it isn't the same thing as a friend's deciding to wade through a snowstorm to help plow me out, or Annie's coming out to serve as midwife in the small hours. Rose's actions arise from a different motive.

The hundreds of times—lambing is just one of many—that Rose served me, stood by me, helped me to achieve the life I wanted, all that gave her a very particular status, to my mind.

Yet I understood what Aquinas was getting at. Rose was not choosing to serve me and do good, not consciously.

So we aren't the same.

Rose can accomplish many feats that I can't; in that sense, she is my superior. But while I can appreciate the good she does for me, she cannot. That is a large part of what distinguishes us from each other.

And yet, so often we share moments when what I need and what she can do fuse perfectly.

Eventually, when lambing was nearly over, the crew completed the HBO Memorial Lambing Pen. A magnificent structure, it never housed a lamb. I wasn't sure what ought to be done with it, and it is now a dormitory for my three goats, but I considered it a monument to Rose, a reminder of that night and so many others when her presence made it possible, literally, for me to live this life.

Sometimes it saddens me that Rose will never truly understand the contribution she's made. Sometimes, though, I'm happy for her, an animal free to do the work her instincts command, relieved of the burden to figure out what's good, who's deserving, and other conundrums that prey on the human mind.

Chapter Seven

THE JEERING GALLERY

A dog has the soul of a philosopher.

—PLATO

I GO OUT TO DO THE BARN CHORES EVERY MORNING, AND AS soon as I open the back door, I am hooted at—by my goats, Murray, Ruth, and Honey.

Their jeering is sharp, loud, a quick nasal *maah* that's impolite and annoying. The goats, short agile beings with furry coats and luminous yellow eyes, a Boer-Saanen cross, inhabit a large pen right behind the house, so they get to see and hear everything.

They're not reserved in their commentary. The cable talk show panelists of the animal world, they're always ready to interject; they have something to say about everything, little of it complimentary. They're the most impertinent animals I know.

They are impish, curious, and, worst of all, bright enough

to carry out their impulses. It is a cardinal principle of farming not to have animals more intelligent than you are. I've already screwed up, because the donkeys are smarter than me. And the goats are smarter than the donkeys, though not nearly as agreeable.

"Nuts to you, goats!" I jeer back each morning. "You don't know anything. Bug off. Be quiet."

They won't be quiet; they can't be. You might as well tell the wind to stop blowing. They don't care what I think, have no desire to please, and their spirits are brimming over with mischief.

The daily ridicule continues as I feed the donkeys, check on the cows, walk the dogs. It abates when I bring the goats the leftover microwaved popcorn I've saved from the previous evening, but resumes when I head for the car.

Goats are not like the other farm residents. Sheep, peaceable creatures, have no interest in me or my activities, unless I'm coming at them accompanied by a border collie or carrying a bale of hay. Even then, once they've been moved to another pasture or polished off the hay, they have little to say.

The cows are even more laissez-faire. If I am bringing them apples or stale Dunkin' Donuts, they appear very concerned about me. Otherwise, they gaze out at other farms, perhaps contemplating the harder fate of other cows; they're not about to move their big bottoms to see what I'm up to.

The donkeys are curious, but also quiet and reflective. They're not rude. I sometimes think I amuse them, but they're discreet enough to keep that to themselves.

My goats, on the other hand, are the farm's Greek chorus, watching me closely and reminding me that I am ridiculous.

Rose has tried several times to herd them. They respond

confoundingly by prancing and playing, and running around in circles. Rose has taken on sheep, cows, other dogs, even pigs, but goats are beyond her authority. They wear her out.

About two years old now, the three all came from the same farm in Shushan, New York. The 4-H'ers who'd raised them passed along this bit of wisdom, regarding their habits: "Sheep eat low, goats eat high."

True enough. Sheep eat grass. Goats eat not only the scrubby brush I hoped they'd clear, they also strip the lower branches of trees I want to survive. That old saw that they'll eat anything? Untrue—when it comes to nonplants, my goats appreciate Paul Newman's low-fat popcorn (including the bag), oat cookies, and Cheerios; they turn up their noses at almost anything else.

The 4-H'ers didn't tell me they mind everybody's business but their own. They stick their noses into your pants pockets. They hop up on rocks, picnic tables, and car hoods. They can open gates, and wriggle under or through fences. Then, having no use for the freedom they've achieved, they hang around, complaining bitterly until you let them back into their pen.

They jeer not only when I'm outdoors, under their scrutiny, but even when I move around inside the house. I hear their contemptuous bleats when I turn on the kitchen light, for instance. Or if I drop a frying pan with a clatter. I sometimes get additional ridicule when I get out of the shower and slam the glass door.

The cows couldn't care less if I'm hauling trash out to the cans. To the goats, it's like a presidential inaugural; they offer a running commentary.

They're always together. Murray is the ringleader, the first one to poke his nose through the wire-mesh fence, the one who kicks off the vituperation, the loudest and most insistent. But Ruth and Honey are not much quieter.

So I've begun jeering back.

GOATS' SPIRITS—part curiosity and intelligence, part refusal to submit to authority—are an odd combination. They're domesticated, useful to humans for eons, but without that sense of service and partnership that dogs have. I'm unable to discern any spiritual bent, the kind donkeys exude. Nor are they contemplative, like cows.

They are virtually untrainable, driven to investigate and disturb. If you don't have a sense of humor, if you're not patient, don't have goats. You'll have to get rid of them, as many people do; I had to let Annie take home an earlier pair of rambunctious Nubians who just didn't fit in, even on a farm called Bedlam. These three are working out better, happily, and that may have as much to do with me as with them.

Goats put us in our places. They're not devoted to serving us, cuddling with us, or meeting our expectations. They are beyond us. Yet they have the gift of making us laugh, during those moments when they are not actively attempting to annoy us.

I'm not proud of the fact that, late in middle age, I'm exchanging insults—largely unfit for a family audience—with these insolent creatures, but there it is.

Unlike dogs, goats are indifferent to what you want or think, almost viscerally incapable of obedience even when it's in their interest.

I admit that I love their imperious personalities, their anti-authoritarianism, their alertness. Surrounded by animals that seem to cherish me—largely because I bring them food—I find it refreshing to have a few that regularly taunt the hand that feeds them.

I wouldn't call them completely without affection. Last spring, I decided to spend some quality time with my goats. I brought some oat cookies, opened the gate, came into their goat pen, sat down at the picnic table that Ruth has turned into her personal Matterhorn.

This was unusual. All three came up to investigate. They nosed me, sniffed my pockets, stared at me as if to say, Just what are you up to? Who do you think you are, anyway? You didn't bring any more than that?

Eventually, Murray and then Ruth put their heads in my hand, even though it was empty. For once they were quiet, practically affectionate. It was nice.

After a few minutes of this uncharacteristic calm, I got up to leave—and was instantly taunted and derided.

"The hell with you, goats!" I yelled back, and went into the house.

Chapter Eight

FLY

Primitive man must tame the animal in himself and
make it his helpful companion; civilized man must
heal the animal in himself and make it his friend.

—CARL JUNG

MY FRIEND SARAH CALLED LAST SPRING TO SAY THAT SHE
thought Fly missed me. You ought to come see her,
she said.

I missed Fly, too. But it was painful to see her. This border collie had known trouble her whole life, and it had been
difficult to let her go. I'd gotten deeply involved in her rescue,
I'd watched her nearly die and then return to life before my
eyes. However one defines soul, ours were joined.

Sarah's farm was just a few miles away. The minute I
walked into the house, Fly came zooming into the room and
threw herself onto the sofa next to me, crawling almost inside
me. I held her for many minutes, kissing her on her nose as
she licked my hands and face.

Animal rescue is very complicated. I'm drawn to it, yet afraid of it. I'm never sure exactly who's being rescued, whether I am doing more for the animal or for myself. I sometimes think the soul of a dog can only be seen in its human mirror—in us, and the boundless way we love these creatures.

When Patsy Beckett, a longtime dog rescuer, first saw Fly tethered to a tree in front of a farmhouse in northern Florida, she pulled her car over for a closer look.

Fly was a gray-and-white border collie of indeterminate age, racing back and forth as much as a short length of clothesline permitted. When border collies don't have real work, they tend to make their own—running fences, chasing cars, obsessing over balls. Untrained and unrestrained, they can become anxious, even a bit mad.

Fly was such a border collie, wild-eyed and wired. Even from the car, Patsy could see that her fur was matted, with bits of dirt and who-knew-what clinging to her coat. The dog was scarecrow-skinny and hyper, dashing one way, then the other.

Most people would have just driven by—hundreds did every day—but it was the sort of scene a dog rescuer notices. Fly's was a breed Patsy often encountered. People get border collies because they're supposed to be smart, then find them too intense, too fixated on work. Such dogs often wind up in deep trouble.

Here we go again, Patsy thought. Why don't I just look the other way this time? Let this one go?

She knew where this would go even before she pulled to the side of the road. Depending on what she saw and how the owner reacted, this border collie would likely join the vast dog rescue underworld, wending her way north.

Over the next few days, Patsy got to know the dog—her neck was wreathed in rope burns, and she had lots of fleas and ticks in her fur and skin—and her suspicious owner. The farmer, when Patsy approached him politely, barked that he'd paid $200 for a watchdog, and no, he wasn't about to put her in a dog run instead of on a rope. And no, he didn't want to sell her. And would this nosey woman please leave his property and mind her own business?

"He didn't want to talk to me," Patsy told me later, with a sigh. She hated these discussions, often tense, with owners. "I didn't get the sense he was cruel, just out of gas. That's often the case with these dogs, really—people are busy, or broke, or just overwhelmed."

But of course Patsy couldn't leave it at that. Fly was outside day and night, in rain, heat, or cold. Apart from the branches of the tree, she had no shelter. She put her head in Patsy's lap when she came, and licked her hand. "She had no reason to love people, but she did," Patsy said.

Patsy also noticed that the dog looked listless and had a disturbing cough, which could mean heartworms. Perhaps there wasn't as much time to wait as Patsy had thought.

She left the owner a few phone messages, again offering to buy the dog or help with vet care; they were never returned. It was becoming unbearable for her to drive by the farm, hard not to think of Fly while she was at work. Patsy was passing the point where she could draw back, remain disengaged.

So, late one evening, Patsy and her friend Jeanine, a member of the same rescue group, parked their creaky Windstar on the road out of sight, crept up to the front lawn, cut Fly's rope with scissors, and walked off with the startled but friendly dog. Patsy's visits had made her no stranger, so the dog didn't bark, and the farmhouse remained dark.

"You will never be treated this way again," Patsy told Fly. "I promise you." They left a note for the farmer, explaining what they'd done and leaving a post-office-box address; he could send a letter if he wanted to be compensated for the dog or was willing to discuss treating her more humanely.

A few hours later, Fly's picture went up on the Web, along with those of thousands of other dogs available for adoption. And I got an email message: Could I help?

THE GROWTH of the dog rescue movement is closely tied to the digital age. Rescuers flourish online. They're obsessive emailers and networkers—it's hard to rescue dogs single-handed—and the growth of the Net has made every dog a national adoptee.

Some of these groups are highly organized, experienced, well funded, and professional. Others are amateur operations run out of garages and backyards.

It says much about the lives dogs lead in America, and about the country itself, that in an age when politicians compete to define how little government should do, there's no comparable rescue movement for people.

Humans who find themselves laid off, in urgent medical trouble, or homeless in America have no such safety net. No van will pull into their driveways to whisk them off to doctors; no one will screen potential homes for them, resettle them with loving caretakers, then visit regularly to make sure they're okay.

But when Fly's rope was cut, she entered an underground that eventually involved individuals and groups from Florida to New York.

She went first to a private home in Jacksonville for a night or two. Meanwhile, messages requesting help and transport were posted on craigslist and Yahoo bulletin boards where dog rescuers congregate and organize.

Next, a "transporter" in a battered old pickup met Fly at an interstate rest stop near Jacksonville and drove her to Atlanta. The better-funded rescue groups can reimburse members for gas and expenses, but most can't. This transporter had spent thousands of her own dollars ferrying dogs.

In Atlanta, she took Fly to a vet tech. Vets vary in their attitudes toward rescue animals; most help when they can, some a lot, some a little. Since few rescuers can afford standard veterinary care, they grow adept at finding alternatives. The lowest-paid of veterinary office staffers, techs attend to sick dogs, collect samples, draw blood, work brutal hours. Yet they're often the most fervent animal lovers in a practice.

In Fly's case, the tech had agreed to tend to rescue dogs at night and on weekends for little or no money. She treated Fly's neck sores, dispensed medication for worms and fleas, vaccinated her against rabies and distemper. A nonprofit mobile veterinary service spayed her for a bargain $60.

As it turned out, though, the would-be helpers nearly killed Fly. Despite repeated warnings from Patsy and me, after we'd consulted our own vets, the mobile service anesthetized Fly without having tested her for heartworm. When the heartbeat slows in a dog with heartworm, the worms cluster around the blood vessels near the heart. The result is often fatal, and even if it doesn't kill the dog, it almost surely weakens the heart and lungs. That's what happened to Fly, apparently inadvertently. Rescuers are almost always well-meaning, but not always saintly, or well organized. Who knew whether our warnings ever reached the people who spayed Fly—or anyone?

Fly then proceeded to Charleston with a different transporter, where another volunteer met her and brought her to a "fosterer."

This Carolina group, I later learned, belonged to a religious sect that didn't believe in traditional medical care, for animals or people. The fosterer treated Fly with herbs, and didn't want to release her without assurances that she wouldn't end up in the hands of conventional vets.

It was starting to look like Fly might have to be rescued from her rescuers. There ensued much emailing, many phone calls, even a discussion with an attorney. Fly disappeared for a week before she was tracked down, then reacquired by conventional rescuers. She resumed her journey north.

Being shuttled about so much can be traumatic for a frightened, unsettled dog. But Fly, who'd been tied to a tree for a long time, seemed to find life on the road interesting. She enjoyed the treats, the attention, the opportunities to chase a Frisbee in the fosterer's yard. Nobody yelled at her. Quite the contrary; everybody loved her.

As volunteer transporters and fosterers passed Fly along, online schedules and notes helped them know what to feed her, how to play with and socialize her. At each stop, people posted progress reports on how her sores and surgical scars were healing, what she liked to eat, what made her nervous. A growing library on Fly was being built daily for her rescuers and, eventually, her new owner.

Fly was being reborn, the reports said. "She has risen," one volunteer gleefully emailed me. She cowered less, and seemed less submissive. She seemed almost to be socializing herself, learning to trust all these nice people. Little remained of her former life; soon she would even acquire a new name.

As she moved about, fosterers evaluated her, checked to

make sure she had no behavioral problems—like aggression, or noise phobias—that would affect where she went. Re-homers and screeners had already begun to grill potential adopters, looking for just the right home. Fly had never lived in a house, apparently, but she liked people. Almost everyone who met her remarked on her sweet, gentle nature. I'm sure many thought of keeping her themselves.

SHE WAS SCHEDULED to arrive at my farm in early spring. My mission was either to integrate her into the existing menagerie here or to find a good home nearby where I could monitor her care.

I met her two hours south of my farm, near the Massa-chusetts border. The call had come from someone describing himself as a musician who traveled to gigs up and down the East Coast. To help pay for his gas and motel bills—and to do something useful and have company—he also transported rescued dogs, for twenty cents a mile. Whenever he headed to an engagement, there was usually a dog or two crated in the back of his Subaru, bound for a new home.

We'd agreed to meet at a restaurant off the Mass Pike. When I found the place, I saw Stan sitting at the wheel, a beautiful gray-and-white border collie in his lap, staring out the window.

We talked for a few minutes, but Stan was eager to be on his way to New Hampshire. So I shook his hand, gave him $50 for his expenses, hooked a leash onto Fly, and coaxed her into my truck. I wanted to get to know this mysterious crea-ture who'd suddenly surfaced in so many people's lives.

I could see she was bright and beautiful, but skittish—common border collie traits. She permitted my pats, then curled up on the floor of the front seat and didn't move until we got back to Bedlam Farm.

Occasionally I offered my hand, and she licked it. I dropped a tiny biscuit every so often; she gobbled them gratefully. But I knew it would be days before I had a clue as to what this dog was like. I could also already see—and hear—that Fly was in trouble.

We went straight to my vet in Salem. The sores around her neck had largely healed; so had the surgical incisions. She was still coughing persistently from the heartworms, however, and her breathing was labored. The vet took blood tests and X-rays and promised to call the next day.

At home, Fly crawled into a crate and didn't come out until the next morning.

Meanwhile, I placed one more call to the farmer from whom Fly had been taken; it seemed the right thing to do.

I told the guy who answered that I now had the dog the rescue group had taken. He said he'd gotten their messages but had no desire to get involved.

"She cost me two hundred dollars," he said, adding that he wouldn't mind being paid.

"You understand why they took the dog?" I asked.

"I guess. I don't mind her being gone, having a better life. I didn't take such good care of her." He sounded a bit embarrassed.

Living upstate these past few years, getting to know neighboring farmers, I had a better sense of how rough his life likely was, how physically taxing his work was, how pressed he might be for time and money. It's easy to be self-righteous about rescuing animals. I told him I'd mail him a check for $200.

NEXT DAY, the vet called with disheartening news: "Fly is a very sick girl. She has category-three heartworm, which is extremely serious."

Because of the anesthesia administered before her spaying, Mary explained, the worms had clustered around her heart. Now she was in real peril; a cluster that broke loose could cause a blockage, even cardiac arrest. Injecting medications to kill the worms would be dangerous, too, with the blood vessels around the heart so swollen. I told Mary I understood the risks and asked her to do the best she could for the dog.

And I began to question whether I could devote the time necessary to nurse Fly back to health and help teach her all the things—from not peeing indoors to walking on a leash—she'd never learned. My schedule on the farm was crazy: lambs coming, the house under repair, my next book due, and a tour looming. Plus, I had my own dogs to worry about.

But I had a friend down the road who kept sheep, goats, and chickens. Sarah had been looking for a dog, and she was the kind of owner rescue groups fantasize about. She was at home every day, spinning and knitting, selling yarn and garments, taking care of her animals.

Nothing made Sarah happier than sitting with an ailing goat all night in the barn; any lamb who even blinked oddly wound up in her kitchen, sucking on a bottle. This could be Fly's happy ending.

But I had to move quickly. Fly was attaching herself to me minute by minute, and vice versa. She'd begun staring at me with her deep, gray-blue eyes, working to figure me out; I was stroking her forty minutes out of every hour. I called Sarah and explained the situation. Sarah had little spare money, I knew, and Fly's treatment would be expensive. I could manage the bills but couldn't spare the time; Sarah had the opposite problems. So I proposed that I see Fly through her medical problems; then, once Fly was healthy, Sarah would take over.

"Bring the dog over," she said. "Let's have a look."

I've been writing for some years now about human-animal attachment, yet I'm often still surprised at the ways in which people and dogs bond.

At Sarah's place, Fly ignored the goats and sheep watching her nervously from behind the pasture fence. Instead, still weak and coughing, she walked slowly into Sarah's living room and curled up at her feet.

Though I know better, it was hard not to believe they'd been waiting for each other. Sarah had left a rugged life back in New England, and like many refugees from urban life, she'd found here a way to reconnect with nature. Fly, a creature who'd never had love or attention, could soak up all that Sarah could provide.

Fly didn't appear to care about sheep or chickens or work at all. After all she'd endured, it was enough for her to find one caring human.

Who knows what's in a dog's mind? But I felt I was seeing this sweet, battered little dog find peace. Perhaps sensing in Sarah a kindred spirit who needed love and was willing to give it.

"You're home now, girl," Sarah told her. I hated letting Fly go, but I knew that Sarah was right.

A few days later, I got this email from her:

"Fly is really adjusting well. We are still thinking we should keep things quiet and make certain that she gets plenty of rest, but it has been nice to see her actually play.

"She has touched us in a way that does not seem possible in such a short time. There is something magical about her. I am charged with providing her with warmth, safety, stability, and love. However, I feel that her presence in our lives has given us a far greater gift than we can ever give her. Can that be possible in such a short time? She is a tiny dog with a huge spirit. We love her. And we love you."

FLY'S SALVATION WAS NOT to be so simple, however. She was still very sick.

She slept almost all day, ate little, coughed whenever she moved quickly. She preferred to stay in her crate, or in Sarah's lap. I've had border collies for years, and it was striking how little this one moved, how indifferent she was to the livestock all around her, how little attention she paid to anything but Sarah.

She began regular blood testing at the vet's. Two weeks after I'd brought her to Sarah, she got a shot of Immiticide— a very strong, and occasionally lethal, drug that kills heartworms and other parasites.

The protocol called for Fly to remain in the veterinary hospital for twenty-four hours, monitored closely to see if she was responding to the treatment. A vet tech agreed to take her home, IV and all, and keep an eye on her through the night.

I dropped Fly off at the clinic that morning. The vets would administer the shot shortly after eight a.m.; I was to call an hour or two later for an update.

Fly pressed her nose against mine. "Be strong, girl," I urged her. "You've come such a long way."

But when I called to see how Fly was doing, the vet told me she was "struggling." I rushed back to the hospital, worrying about Fly, and now also about Sarah, who already loved the dog so dearly that her loss would be extraordinarily painful. I would feel awful about bringing these two together, over such a long distance at such great expense and trouble, only to make them both suffer so.

Fly did look dreadful, drooling and writhing in her crate, clearly in pain. One of the vets told me to call Sarah and prepare her.

I could tell Sarah sensed the pessimism in my voice; she began to cry. "She's struggling, Sarah," I said. "The vets still think she might pull through, but you need to be ready." I almost couldn't bear it. After all this dog had been through, how could she die in a crate at a vet's office?

I knew this vet well; she was competent, compassionate, and direct. When she asked if I knew whether Sarah would want Fly's body buried or cremated, she was telling me something.

At such moments the extraordinary relationship between humans and dogs comes to life. It has created a new ethical consciousness. The idea that animals should not ever be killed, and that we ought to prolong their lives at great expense for long periods of time, is as new as it is startling, even profound.

Our love of animals like dogs is causing us to redefine our relationship with another species.

It is a social and cultural phenomenon, a mirror of our society. We have to consider how much we love them. What is their place in our lives? How much do they mean to us? How much can we afford to spend on their care? Is there a point where we should let them go? How much grieving will we do, should we do, and why?

The bond between people and their animals is no longer simple, if it ever was. It reflects a growing view of dogs and cats and other animals as being like us—better, even, than us. For some, it defines how good we are, how loving and faithful.

People say, more and more, that their dogs and cats are members of the family, not really pets. If they say it, it becomes true, and if it is true, it raises all sorts of new challenges for us. If our dogs have souls, deciding their fates is not as easy as it used to be. Putting an animal down is one thing. Killing a member of the family is quite another.

I know a farmer who lives near me who had a border collie he loved and who served him faithfully for fourteen years. One morning the dog came up lame and hobbled into the kitchen. The farmer turned to his wife and said, "Honey, say goodbye to Demon."

"Why?" she asked.

"Because I'm going to take him out into the barn and shoot him."

The farmer's wife, recounting the story later, said she was very sad, because she loved Demon a great deal. But there was no questioning the decision, she added quickly. You don't keep a lame dog on a farm.

This new relationship explains the intensity of the rescue culture, the deep feelings these powerless animals spark in us. "C'mon, girl," I pleaded with Fly, who lay near death in the surgical suite. "You didn't come all this way to die here. You can get through."

I opened her crate and Fly crawled over toward me, pulling her IV tube along with her. I suddenly wished I had kept her myself, so that if she died I could have spared Sarah this blow. But losing Fly would be a blow for me, too. I'd identified with this dog months ago, when I first heard about her.

Fly's condition seesawed through the day, her fever soaring, then abating. I stayed nearby and phoned Sarah with updates, mostly grim. Then in late afternoon, as I was trying to catch a bit of sleep in my truck, a tech came and tapped on the window. Fly's fever had finally ebbed. She was looking more alert. The vets said her heart and other vital signs seemed normal.

Kris, one of the staff, took Fly home with her that night. Like all of us, she'd come to dote on this gentle creature, and she slept with Fly next to her, her hand on the dog's heart to be sure it kept beating. Late that night, as I'd asked, Kris called me.

"She's doing great," she said. "Amazing turnaround. She's alert, drinking, licking me." In turn, I called Sarah, who burst into tears at this surprising news. I was relieved, but still cautious; the dog I'd spent the day with was anything but healthy.

Fly went home to Sarah's the next day. She needed crate rest and leash walking for weeks, and her treatments would continue for months: more injections, a steady diet of steroids and anti-inflammatories and antibiotics. The shots themselves caused pain and soreness, chronic diarrhea, fatigue, and nausea. The bills climbed past $1,300, which is where the rescue culture meets the real world. How many dogs, however poignant their stories, can be saved at such steep price tags?

She never fully recovered her strength. She still tired easily, especially for a border collie, although over the next few months, her stamina increased. She did develop some of the strange and obsessive habits of the breed, staring for hours at

Sarah's guinea hens. As her appetite returned, she figured out how to open kitchen cabinets.

She's never learned herding, though, or showed much interest in sheep. Sarah loves nurturing wounded things, but she's not drawn to training. So while Fly will happily stare at beavers in the creek or chickens in the yard, she seems afraid of larger animals and backs away from them.

Hers is a happy human-meets-dog story, nonetheless. Fly attaches herself to Sarah's ankle much of the day. When Sarah does her barn chores, Fly follows along. When she sits out in her studio, spinning yarn, knitting hats and sweaters, Fly curls up between her and the woodstove.

FLY IS NOTHING if not innocent, responsible neither for her troubles nor for her subsequent good fortune. Her life is as good as human beings decide to make it; she can only go along for the ride. She can never be truly aware of the good done on her behalf, though I know many animal lovers would disagree.

The day may come, philosopher Jeremy Bentham wrote two centuries ago, when animals acquire those rights that should never have been withheld from them, except for humans' arrogance and tyranny. I don't know if he's right, or if that would be an unqualified good thing.

Bentham rejected a number of Aristotelian notions about human superiority. A full-grown horse or dog is decidedly more rational than any infant, he believed. And he wrote about our obligations to treat animals morally.

"The question," he wrote of animals, "is not, Can they *reason*? Nor Can they *talk*? But, Can they *suffer*?"

They can, of course, and I don't doubt that Fly had. Taking her in, loving her, was a moral opportunity, a way for me to perform an act of compassion.

When people meet Fly, or when I tell them about her, I see the warmth in their faces, and hear their words of praise (for me) and sympathy (for her). I feel approved of. "Thank you for the wonderful work that you do," one vet tech told me during my many visits to check on Fly.

But the praise, generously intended, makes me uncomfortable, too. I remember leaving the clinic thinking that the tech had spoken to me the same way someone might have spoken to Mother Teresa or some other humanitarian, and as I climbed into my truck, I remember thinking, Katz, you are no Mother Teresa. The "wonderful work" involved mostly making phone calls, writing checks, and driving a dog around.

This is part of what made me uneasy about rescue.

Bentham is right to see the treatment of animals as a moral issue, a matter of ethics, not just laws.

But the rescue and treatment of animals, in our time, are seen so *much* as moral issues that stories like Fly's raise real questions. I meet people almost daily who tell me their dogs or other animals were abused, and many who feel strongly that rescuing a dog is the only morally acceptable way to acquire one.

While many animals *are* severely abused, a number of studies have found that animal abuse tends to be overdiagnosed and overreported, and occurs less frequently than many animals lovers believe, notes Steven R. Lindsay in his comprehensive *Handbook of Applied Dog Behavior and Training*. Shelter and rescue workers know that "abused" dogs are much more likely to be adopted than those merely lost or abandoned. Often adopters—people like me—seem to feel that kind treatment of needy animals makes them righteous people.

Fly unlocked a response in me, something I'd been circumspect of, something that I now consciously seek to limit. It felt good to rescue her, pleasurable. But I don't feel entirely at ease about the status animals have in my life, or in our society.

So many animals are in need, and there are no clear boundaries on how many are too many for one person to manage, or how much effort animals should command compared to the efforts we make to help human beings.

The "rescue" element of acquiring animals can be psychologically and emotionally challenging, sometimes intense, especially if the people engaged in it are unaware of their own psychological backstories and motivations.

I'm leery of a life with animals in which the rescue becomes an end in itself, more important than the dog or cat or cow; in which I have more animals than I can know and understand and care for well. It's easy to spend all day running to vets, preparing special diets, cleaning up messes, dispensing pills, and applying bandages. The need is infinite, the boundaries fuzzy.

I don't want to rescue animals primarily because I want to feel better about myself, or better than some other people, or morally superior to anyone. The best part of my life with animals is the humility they teach, the humanity they foster.

I've seen that some people deeply involved in animal rescue can be self-righteous, with harsher views of their fellow humans than of dogs. It's easy to feel virtuous, harder to be aware of one's own self-interest.

So I try to limit the number of animals I bring onto the

farm and into my life. And I try hard to be aware of my own motives.

I've even grown wary of the word "rescue." It can signal a glib, self-serving perspective. I not only "rescued" Fly but, after her, Izzy and Emma, more border collies from a local abandoned farm. And Elvis the steer, in a way, and then Harold and Luna. I could call Winston a rescued rooster, I suppose. I've been directly or indirectly involved in the re-homing of scores of dogs, cats, and farm animals in recent years.

It's become too charged a word.

Izzy is not a rescued animal, in my eyes, not a piteous creature whose presence ennobles me. Like many animals (and people), he had difficult times and deserved better. He used to live there, and now he lives here. His past no longer really matters, surely not to him; the only reason for invoking it is to serve myself.

Izzy, like so many animals, is unscathed and happy to move on, with no reason or capacity to see himself as having been saved. It's a good lesson: Doing better for animals is satisfying and meaningful, but so is doing better for people.

Bringing animals to my farm or to other good homes makes me someone who wants to do good, but also someone who was wounded, in some ways broken, and who now seeks to salve his wounds through the involuntary use of unknowing animals who have no choice in the matter, no ability to elect to be elsewhere. As Aristotle pointed out so long ago, animals have no free will.

Fly benefited from my need to rescue her, as did other dogs. I know that Fly can suffer, and so can I; there, perhaps, is where animal and human meet.

But truth matters, too.

It's a lovely thing to take in an animal, but it does not make me moral. It's merciful to give a dog who needs one a home, but it's hardly a selfless act.

To treat animals well and ease their suffering, to see animals as being in need of protection and as having some elemental rights makes moral sense to me. But it's at least as ethical to ease the suffering of our own species.

I'm pleased to have transported Fly to a new home, to have treated her illness. Was I doing good for a dog, or doing good for me? I think I know the answer: for both of us, always for both.

Chapter Nine

ROSE AND MY SOUL

There is no faith which has never yet been broken,
except that of a truly faithful dog.

—KONRAD LORENZ

KEN NORMAN, THE FARRIER, WAS COMING TO TRIM THE
donkeys, and as usual he didn't give me much notice. It
doesn't matter. Farriers are important, and there aren't too
many of them.

I had to scramble to separate the sheep from the donkeys,
get the donkeys into a small room in the big barn where they
couldn't fight too hard, keep them inside, get hay to them to
keep them still, and keep the sheep out.

Sheep and donkeys do not understand the notion of separate tasks and individual food, and wild brawls can break out
when grain is used to entice animals like donkeys inside a
barn—the only way I can get them there. The sheep want the
grain, and will battle for it, and they, too, will want to come

into the barn. And then one of the sheep was coughing badly and I had called the Granville Large Animal Veterinary Service, and they also were on the way.

That meant I had to isolate the ewe, get her into her own stall in the barn, and keep her there. Sheep do not like to be alone, and I couldn't give this one any company, as she was sick. It was going to be one of those continuing dramas that some farm people call chores. They are all unnerving, even a bit frightening, but they usually seem to work out. You have to stay calm.

There was a time in my life, and it is fairly recent, when I had as much to do with a farrier as with a Russian cosmonaut circling the moon, and I could not imagine moving sheep and donkeys in and out of barns, nor had I a clue as to how to do it.

These days, after some years on the farm, I know how to do it. "Rosie, let's get to work," I yelled.

If Bedlam Farm had a theme song, that would be it. I "sang" it the first night we arrived, when the animals broke through the fence and ran out into a blizzard, and Rose got them back, and I have been singing it ever since.

I have all sorts of commands I give to the dogs every day—Let's take a walk, Let's go to the woods, Let's go take photos, Let's take a ride—but there is one particular command that is only for Rosie, and she absolutely lives to hear it: "Rosie, let's go to work."

It's like a bugler sounding the charge for the cavalry. Wherever Rose is, she materializes at the nearest door, head low, eyes intense, all business. Usually, it's at the back door, the one nearest the animal pastures.

Rose waits, nose to the door, while I put on my boots and then open the door. She shoots into the back of the house, down to the pasture gate, and is waiting for me impatiently by the time I lumber up. She never knows exactly what the task is on a given day.

She is not a herding dog per se, the kind you see in trials or on TV, but a working farm dog, and she constantly watches me for cues and clues about her mission. When there is work with Rose, there is no messing around. She gets it done. The rest of the world—people, food, other dogs—recedes, vanishes. She concentrates, focuses, pays attention. She is bright. She is brave. She is tireless. She is wired into me, fused almost, and knows what I want her to do, and means to do it. She hears my voice, watches my eyes, senses my mood, reads my mind.

Today, it is a bit more complicated than usual, but it never takes her too long to figure it out. And I never doubt that she will get it, and do it, because she always does and has. Sometimes I feel that we are not two things, man and dog, but one.

Rose rushes up to the pasture, then turns to me, awaiting instructions. "Get the donkeys," I say. Rose and the donkeys are not crazy about each other. The donkeys, ever protective of the sheep, often challenge Rose when she goes to herd them, and Lulu and Fanny have each kicked her once or twice. She responds by nipping both of them on the butt from time to time to keep them in line. Rose will not be deterred.

They have an uneasy truce, but when she needs to get them to do something, they usually end up doing it.

She rushes up behind Jeannette, the donkey leader, and lunges at her leg, causing Jeannette to turn and move toward me. Jeannette is a wise old girl, and she never wants to tangle with this crazy and relentless dog. As she moves down to me, Jesus and Fanny follow, as donkeys don't like to be alone any more than sheep do, especially with Rose. Lulu, ever independent, hangs back. "Look back," I yell to Rose, a command to round up stragglers, and she charges up behind Lulu, and nips at her tail.

Donkeys are willful and independent, but they don't much like trouble, and Lulu comes skittering down to join the rest of us. I go into the barn, get some grain, shake it into a cup. That's all the donkeys need to hear. I slide open the barn door, walk with the cup into the room where the trimming will be done, and the donkeys follow. I will toss some hay in to keep the donkeys occupied.

As I expected, the sheep have heard the grain in the cup and are making a lot of noise, gathering and heading for the barn. I tell Rose to lie down, permitting the sheep to charge down toward me.

Normally, she would not permit this, but in a lie-down, they will move past her, and when they do, I point to the sick ewe and tap it on the head, and Rose charges in, isolating the ewe and two others and backing them away from the flock, which takes off up the hill, and holding them near me. I slide open the barn door and, with Rose on the other side of the three sheep, they rush into the barn.

With the crook, I drag the sick ewe into the holding pen next to the donkeys, whose gate has been left open. The donkeys are ready for the farrier, the ewe is ready for the vet. I call Rose—I always have to call her several times, as she hates to leave work—and we go back into the house. I turn on the computer and go to work. I can imagine getting through a day without Rose—I just can't imagine how I would survive.

EVERYONE I ASK who loves a dog tells me their dog has a soul, and they haven't much doubt about it. I think they are really telling me something about their own souls. The dogs are never participating. They don't really need to talk about souls, and neither do the donkeys, cows, or sheep.

My animals, especially the dogs, live in the now. Their lives are elemental. They worry about food, and the life and smells around them. They worry about me, and I think perhaps they worry about each other. I do not believe they worry about their spirits or afterlives. Right after I got Rose I began to live my life. I moved upstate, bought this farm, confronted some personal issues, began taking photographs, made amazing friends, found my sister, discovered the meaning of love, got help.

Rose helped make that life possible and, in some ways, came to define it. She gave me strength. She provided support. We stood side by side through blizzards, animal dramas, lambings, quarrelsome rams, renegade donkeys, feral rabid cats, wild pigs, lonely days and nights.

I don't honestly know if I could have made it without her, but I don't believe that I could have, which is what is perhaps most important.

I need Rose to be Rose. I could not have survived that first awful winter on the farm, a winter of storms, ice, and bitter cold, and the strange and demanding life of a farm without Rose, or without the idea of her.

When I had to charge outside at three a.m. and saw the thermometer at minus 20, it was the idea of Rose charging ahead of me, leading the way, finding the sheep, getting to the lambs, that gave me the heart to do it. I knew that whatever happened to these animals—breaking through the fence, fighting over grain, bumping into me, needing medical care—Rose would help me figure it out, help me do it. And she did.

I don't believe that on some of those winter nights when I fell down on the hard ice, and knocked myself out and she nipped on my ear and barked until I stood up, that I would have always gotten up otherwise.

I don't know whether I would have had the strength or the courage to live on this remote hill, beset by coyotes, falling wires, broken water pipes, rotting fences, collapsing barns, lightning strikes and storms, and the relentless responsibilities of running a farm, caring for animals, and staying strong. When I couldn't see, Rose was always watching.

When I couldn't run fast enough, Rose got there.

When I was afraid, Rose was determined.

When I was confused, she was sure.

I didn't know what to do about a charging ram, but Rose did. I didn't know how to get a runaway donkey back into the fence. Rose always knew. I couldn't fathom how to keep the donkeys and sheep from fighting over grain, and knocking me down, but Rose always kept order.

I was worried about getting sick sheep into the barn until the vet arrived, but Rose wasn't worried, and got them there. She always seemed to know what to do.

I couldn't imagine moving sheep through the woods to find a new pasture, but Rose always got them there. For six years, day and night, hot and cold, sun or storm, Rose has watched over me and this farm, and the animals in it, and never once failed to do what she needed to do, or know what she needed to do, giving me the strength and confidence, and eventually the experience, to be here and live my life.

Her soul and mine are not really separate, one completes the other, and it isn't just about love, either—although that is a perfectly good bond. I came to the farm to live, to free my soul—to have a soul—and I believe in my heart that I could not have done this without that humorless and purposeful creature.

That's my story, and I've been telling it for some time now. It's a good story.

I suppose it's not entirely true, although I still believe it and tell it in good faith. The story of Rose gives me the strength to live my life, and that counts for something. A lot. Looking back on it, it isn't that I think it's false, but that I understand better why I came up with it. I am much too fearful a person to have come up to the farm by myself.

As I look around me, I see that people survive without Rose; in fact, most farms don't have Rose. They manage. I suppose I could manage.

I have come to see that Rose does not need to have a soul, or need to think about one. I need for her to have one.

IN THE AUTUMN of my life, I am fighting for my life, still and forever, and at each struggle, each turning point, a dog has appeared to take me where I needed to go, and to keep my spirits strong.

A dog guided me to the farm. A dog helped me live here. A dog connected me to the lives and spirits of human beings around me. A dog helped me learn to love.

Does this mean that dogs have souls, or does it mean we create the dogs we need, seek them out, reinforce them, and project our needs onto them? I think I am coming to see it, at last. It is not a cynical idea, this idea of mine, but a loving one. Dogs are very important to me.

Izzy has the soul I want him to have, give him the opportunity to have. He enriches me. At a time when I was still learning how to love, Lenore helped show me how to love.

Rose, of all my dogs, fulfills the glorious history of dogs

in service to human beings, completing them, helping them lead the lives they want and need to live.

Dogs and humans have an elaborate way of communicating with one another, and one of the things that makes it so complex is its inequality. We have narrative, language, and history. They have instincts and senses beyond our imagination. They are aware of our emotions, moods, smells, impulses; and their ability to thrive and survive is based partly on their canny skills at reading and manipulating us.

If we are happy, they know it, and respond to it. If we are angry, they grow anxious. They have no direct language with which to talk to us, yet their ability to know what we like and want is hardwired and finely and richly honed.

I can't honestly separate what people need of dogs from the souls of dogs. My instincts are just not strong enough. I am not sure enough. I have learned that there are many things I just don't know and will never know. Much of the interaction between dogs and people is a mystery to me, beyond me. I know that dogs are not inferior to us; their instincts far surpass any of ours.

One of the most compelling theories about dogs and their consciousness comes from psychologist David Premack of the University of Pennsylvania and is called the "theory of mind." It says that we are self-aware and conscious, and that other creatures are also self-aware and self-conscious; also, we must recognize that these other creatures may have their own points of view and mental processes, and that these might be the same or different from our own.

When Rose looks to see which shoes I put on so that she can know if we are going to work, she is showing an awareness of me, beyond her own reality. When Lenore goes up and hops into bed at night, anticipating that I will soon join her, she is stepping out of herself, and is aware of my behavior. When Izzy goes into a bedroom and finds a dying patient and comforts him, he is showing awareness of another being.

These examples abound in my life. When Elvis comes to the gate and bellows when I go upstairs into my study; when the donkeys bray greetings when I get up in the morning and put my feet on the floor; when the sheep head for the pasture gate when they see Rose and me come out the back door. All of these things tell me that as I am aware of them, animals are aware of me. But this does not mean we are the same thing, with the same aspirations. I worry about my soul, but there is no reason to suppose Rose worries about hers, surely not in the same language and context that I might.

In *How Dogs Think,* the famed behaviorist Stanley Coren writes that "dogs seem to be very aware of the fact that other individuals have a particular point of view that must be taken into account." I have found this to be true. They are keenly aware of us, in ways few of us really grasp or appreciate.

I have always found it a little demeaning to put our words into the minds of animals. I don't need or want them to be like me. They are better than that. They have their own kind of language, their own consciousness.

I find questions concerning loyalty, empathy, and intuitiveness closer to getting at what animals might really be feeling, or sensing. I see those traits all the time. When I am sick, Rose will not leave my side voluntarily, not to eat, go out, eliminate. What is she sensing? What is she doing?

I don't know. I know that I will never know.

Mostly, what my dogs need is me. My love, direction, and commitment, which give them the opportunity to live their lives to the fullest extent possible, as I wish to live mine. In this way, we complement one another.

————

AS I WRITE THIS, Rose is sitting in my study, moving from one window to another, checking to see where the donkeys are, where the sheep are, if any coyotes or stray dogs have turned up, if there is trouble, if alarms should be sounded, work should be done.

She doesn't offer me a lot of love in the traditional sense. She doesn't want to cuddle or sleep in bed with me, or need a lot of treats or fussing. She lives in service to me, gives herself over to the life I want and need to have.

In that way, she is a critical part of my soul, and I cannot really find the difference between hers and mine.

And it doesn't really matter to me. My dogs are well beyond the spiritual fussing of humans. I think sometimes that they can see us but we can't really see them beyond our own needs and projections. For sure, we are needier than they are.

Chapter Ten

LULU GOES TO HELL

God made the wild animals according to their kinds, the livestock according to their kinds, and all the creatures that move along the ground according to their kinds. And God saw that it was good.

Then God said, "Let us make man in our image, in our likeness, and let him rule over the fish of the sea and the birds of the air, over the livestock, over all the earth, and over all the creatures that move along the ground."

—Genesis 1:25–26

HENRY WHITFIELD CLIMBED OUT OF THE AGING IMPALA, offered me his hand, patted my shoulder, and handed me a jug of cider as a gift.

He always looked out of place anywhere but in church. He wore a blue parka over black slacks and a white dress shirt, with a fur hat. I suspected there was a black suit jacket in his car, plus a sober tie. He carried a pair of rubber boots in a

brown paper bag, in case we ventured into the barn or pasture.

We'd first gotten to know each other, via email, a few
years ago when I wrote about Thomas Merton, the late author and well-known Trappist monk. I'd visited Henry's
church in central New York State once or twice, too, heard
him preach and conduct services, and we'd become friendly.
I invited him to come by when he was passing through, heading to Lake George on vacation or to visit friends in Canada.
I'd made several friends who were deeply religious since
moving upstate, and I'd come to value their perspective. It
was pleasant, when Henry came by, to trade some spiritual
chatter and stories about our lives, and to stroll around the
farm.

"The new barn looks beautiful," said Henry on this brisk
afternoon, taking in the changes since his last visit. He had
the air, today, of someone with business to conduct, more
like an insurance adjuster than a pal who'd come to hang
around. "You look well, and I hope you are well. Let's talk
about this animals and souls business."

I'd called to ask for his counsel. I was exploring the idea of
the souls and spirits of animals, I explained, and even though
my inquiry wasn't religious, exactly, religious questions came
up from time to time. As I talked more about what I'd been
reading and puzzling over, he nodded. He got it.

I always found him to be a clear thinker, with enormous
conviction, yet eager to absorb other points of view. He
seemed willing to hear me out, even when he didn't agree.

I saw no evidence that Henry was crazy about animals;
tending to people was his passion, and he seemed quite good
at it. I could use his clarity, I thought, on a subject so clouded
by emotion.

Henry had a funeral to preside over that evening, he said, explaining the shirt and dress slacks. He'd put 150,000 miles on his noisy, rusting car, driving to baptisms and weddings, calling on the ill, lonely, or spiritually adrift members of his congregation.

Izzy, always hoping to charm fresh admirers, came over as we spoke and put his head in Henry's hand. Henry patted him politely, in the way of people who want to be gracious but aren't really enthusiastic.

"New dog?" he asked. "He's cute." But he didn't seem to want to hear Izzy's story, all the details of how he'd come to me.

"He's going to heaven, isn't he?" I asked jokingly as we walked toward the big dairy barn I'd just restored.

Henry shook his head. So we were into it already.

"Really?" I said sadly. "But he's such a good guy."

"He's very nice," Henry agreed, striding purposefully toward the donkeys. "But there is only one way to get to heaven, one ticket in, and that's accepting Jesus Christ as Lord and Savior. If you accept Christ, you go to heaven. If you don't, I'm afraid, you don't."

Henry, it turned out, wasn't terribly interested in hearing what Aristotle had to say about animals, nor the ideas of the minister down the hill from me who assured me that God made and loved all his creatures and would surely not exclude our pets from heaven.

The Bible, Henry said, was quite clear. "Lots of ministers want their congregants to be happy," he said. "And so do I. But wanting something to be true doesn't make it so. Animals cannot, so far as I know, accept Jesus. They are not like us." And he quoted the passage from Genesis I've partly reprinted here.

This passage is important; it established the notion, widely held in the Western world, that humans have dominion over animals, that God created animals to serve us, and clearly intended for us to rule over them.

It's shaped much of the relationship between so-called civilized people and animals, determined the fates of countless creatures. Animals are clearly not our equals, according to Genesis; they are something less, something apart.

Certainly that's how Henry read it. "The Scriptures are clear," he said. "We have dominion over the animals, over all the creatures that move along the ground.

"One woman in my congregation said to me, 'But Reverend Henry, I love my cat more than my husband. Surely you are not telling me that he won't have eternal life, that he doesn't have a soul.' "

Henry paused to look around, and noticed Elvis gazing hopefully at him over the pasture gate. Where there was a paper bag, there might be apples or carrots or a Snickers bar.

"Well," Henry said, "that is a large cow."

What about the woman who worried about her cat's soul?

"I said, 'Sorry, Charlene, I wish I had better news for you, but there are no shortcuts to heaven, no exceptions, I'm afraid, not even for your cat.' "

Henry pulled his rubber boots from his bag and, leaning against a fencepost, exchanged them for his dress shoes. Even in the boots, he looked a bit odd. "You look all shiny and pressed, like an undertaker," I kidded him. "Not like us rumpled and disheveled farm types."

He laughed. "You look appropriately rumpled and disheveled," he said. "You look the part now, limp and all. You've grown into yourself."

We opened the gate, and entered the pasture. I thought Lulu might soften the Reverend Whitfield up a bit.

LULU IS MY MOST CALM and affectionate donkey, with irresistible wide brown eyes, long lashes, and a soft warm nose. She likes contact with people, and is so gentle that newcomers quickly overcome any nervousness. If you sit down near her, she comes over and places her head on your shoulder, or nuzzles you with her cheek. She's probably the farm's most soothing presence, who's never harmed anyone or anything.

When people tell me they can't imagine how their animals could be excluded from heaven, I think of Lulu, the way she radiates gentleness. Her eyes seem to contain the wisdom and understanding that donkeys have amassed from their thousands of years serving humanity.

I handed Henry a cookie and suggested he give it to Lulu. He held it out in the palm of his hand as if it were radioactive, and Lulu slowly drifted over, carefully took the cookie, enjoyed it, and pressed her head against his shoulder. She was waiting for a scratch.

Henry patted the top of her fuzzy head a few times, while I pointed out the cross emblazoned on her back, the rich history of donkeys, the many references to them in both Jewish and Christian theology. He smiled a bit.

Then he leaned forward and looked her in the eyes. "Lulu," Henry said softly, "do you accept Jesus Christ as your Lord and Savior?"

Lulu snorted, rubbed her nose against Henry's hat.

He turned to me. "She is not going to heaven," he said. "Sorry."

She seemed to take the news with the equanimity for

which donkeys are justly famous, and edged closer to me. Perhaps I had a cookie, or better news.

Henry laughed. He enjoyed being a messenger of God, a teller of the truth—the truth as he understood it, rather than the truth people might prefer to hear. His was a fixed creed in a world where people tried on beliefs like sweaters. He knew who he was, what he was supposed to do, what his job was. It was not to cater to the animal adoration he saw around him.

Not that he didn't love animals, Henry explained. Not that they weren't important. God had made it clear that they were. He quoted from Job 12:10: " 'In his hand is the life of every creature and the breath of all mankind.' " It called on humans to love and respect all creatures.

"Think of it, 'the breath of all mankind,' " Henry said. "That's an important message, because it says to me that the breath of all mankind is in every living thing and that *his hand* is in the life of every creature. So the animals are sacred, and we should treat them with love and mercy and respect. Your animals are sacred to me because *his hand* is in them all."

Nevertheless, he went on, the Lord gave us dominion over them, and he gave us the means to choose between good and evil, and thus to have souls, which ascend to heaven—or not.

"Are you telling me that Lulu is going to hell?" I asked, now a bit concerned.

Henry smiled. "I don't know. Maybe. I think not. She can't accept Christ, so she can't be punished for not accepting him," he said. "I don't believe God would punish animals for acting in the very way he intended when he created them. But we ought not to judge animals the way we judge ourselves. They cannot do good or bad."

Wasn't it possible, I asked, as we left my possibly doomed donkeys and headed over to see Elvis and Harold and Luna, that because God and Jesus both loved and appreciated animals, they would allow them to join people in heaven? If they are sacred, aren't they too precious to be left behind?

"Anything is possible," said Henry. "And I don't mean to be arrogant. But I believe the Bible is the Word, and it is unambiguous: We have dominion over them. There's nothing in the Bible about animals having souls, being rewarded, or having eternal life." However precious or beloved animals are, he maintained, humans can't alter God's word simply because they love their pets.

I appreciated what Henry was saying, and admired his consistency and integrity. It was a relief, though, that I wasn't especially religious, not as scripturally bound as he was, and therefore freer to consider other possibilities. Not that I had any answers either.

Henry wasn't bending with the prevailing winds, swaying along with modern theologians, or comforting fervent animal lovers who find it incomprehensible that their pets won't enjoy life beyond their physical beings.

"I don't mean to upset people who love animals, but faith is faith," Henry says. "And belief is not always convenient to the tides of the moment."

He and I usually skirted questions about my own faith. I was raised a Jew, became a Quaker, have flirted with some early versions of Christianity, and am now a strange blend of all three, plus a healthy dose of secularity. One day, I hope to get these matters sorted out, but that hasn't happened yet.

Henry has made it clear that if I don't accept Jesus as the son of God, then I'm destined for hell, whether Lulu is there or not. He said—only once—"The door is always open to you, you know." And I do.

But though we have differing views on souls, faith, and animals, I can't fault him—quite the opposite—for staying true to his beliefs, reminding me that with faith comes sacrifice, and that faith shouldn't be subject to the latest public-opinion poll.

Still, dogma can be rigid, even cold, and people who study the Bible can find support for a hundred different points of view. Many theologians believe that there's plenty of room in the Gospels for animals.

A friend had given me *The Bible Promise Book,* a volume full of uplifting quotations. I'd found a reading from the Gospel of John (10:27–28) that seemed apropos, and I'd copied it down and pulled it out of my pocket to show Henry: "My sheep listen to my voice; I know them, and they follow me. I give them eternal life, and they shall never perish; no one can snatch them out of my hand."

I don't love sheep as much as John does, nor do I think mine are headed for eternal life. But if John is promising his flock eternal life, then there's hope for Lulu, right? Perhaps Henry was drawing the requirements too narrowly.

I don't know; I'm not a theologian. One of the things I love most about animals is that they're *not* dogmatic or litigious. Staking out positions about their capacities and their care, on the other hand, often triggers anger, self-righteousness, and moral superiority, traits animals themselves clearly don't possess.

I read the passage proudly, but of course I had underestimated Henry and wandered in well over my head.

The author of the passage, Henry pointed out patiently,

was the fisherman John, Jesus' most beloved disciple, and was quoting Jesus at the temple when he said that his sheep (meaning his human followers, not literal animals) know him and follow him, as a flock follows its shepherd. Henry smiled, and put one arm around my shoulder. He was expressing his love of people, not sheep.

So my sheep aren't bound for heaven, either, it seems.

Although I was joking, sort of, the idea of the shepherd has particular relevance for me. Herding sheep with Rose is probably one of the most spiritual things I do, partly because it's such a time-honored practice, partly because the figure of the protective, watchful shepherd is so deeply embedded in religious lore.

Acceptance of Jesus was the only way to eternal life, in his book and in his Book, but Henry understood the impulse to think otherwise. "People love animals so much that they want to give them this gift, which is a beautiful thing," he said.

And he countered with a quote from Matthew (10:29–31): " 'Are not two sparrows sold for a penny? Yet not one of them will fall to the ground apart from the will of your Father. And even the very hairs of your head are all numbered. So don't be afraid: you are worth more than many sparrows.' "

Lots of people in this country, I told Henry, seem to believe that animals are equal or superior to humans. That dogs are more pure and loving, and far less destructive. It makes sense to them that animals actually *deserve* to go to heaven more than many people do.

We were in the cow pasture now, where Elvis was eyeing Henry expectantly, hoping more for a Snickers than eternal life.

"Well, this is the heart of it, isn't it?" asked Henry, wrapping his scarf tightly around his neck and taking out his gloves. "God loves the people he created, and he loves them above all things. God loves animals, too, and the flowers and the mosquitoes and flies, but he loves his children the most. He gave only them the gift of good and the challenge of evil, and the most precious part of the soul—the choice between the two."

It demeans both people and animals, he said, to equate them and say that both have immortal souls. It borders on blasphemy. It is simply not so, however disappointed we are in ourselves, or smitten with the animals in our lives.

We opened the pasture gate and I went in to offer Elvis a potato, which he began to crunch on, still eyeing Henry.

"That is a large animal," Henry said again, wading over gingerly in his boots to scratch the side of Elvis's nose. Elvis appreciated the scratching, and drooled on Henry's glove.

The Bible was full of references to huge beasts of burden, Henry said, and there was definitely something biblical about Elvis.

"Elvis, you are a gentle creature and a dumb beast," he announced. "Jon wants you to go to heaven, but I can't give you that. I can bless you, though, and all of the animals here."

It was a lovely thought. I didn't remind Henry that I was not certain there was a heaven at all, for humans or for Elvis. My interest in animals and souls was more secular than religious.

BUT WHEN HENRY CLOSED HIS EYES and bowed his head, I followed suit, feeling a surge of affection for this conscientious man who'd taken the trouble to drive out to my farm on a freezing day on a somewhat hopeless mission to set us all straight.

A cold wind whistled down the pasture hill, but the sky was bright, almost painfully blue. I saw that the donkeys had come over to their side of the fence and were watching with interest. Rose was up in the far pasture, moving the sheep here and there, and Izzy was following us around, observing.

Henry raised his arm, as if to embrace my farm: "Which of all of these does not know that the hand of the Lord has done this? In his hand is the life of every creature, and the breath of all mankind. Amen." He held his hand up, signaling me not to interrupt.

" 'Open your mouth for the dumb, for the rights of all that are left desolate,' " he added. "Proverbs 31:8. I thought I might need it."

We had some tea together inside the farmhouse and talked of other things. I thanked him for coming, and he invited me to services at his church. I said I would drop by.

HENRY'S MESSAGE, which I mulled for a few hours before I got it, wasn't intended to dismiss the animal world. Though his beliefs weren't open to debate, he thought the real question wasn't whether animals could enter heaven; it was whether we loved them and treated them well. Here he and I could find comfortable common ground.

"Animals are especially deserving," he had said as we warmed up indoors, "because they cannot ask for mercy."

I worried a bit for him, envying his great clarity about his faith, yet feeling he was also somewhat out of sync with the times and with many of his own congregants.

Still, his talk reminded me of something Andrew Linzey had said in *Animal Gospels.* Even though his view of animals and souls was different from Henry's, there was common ground there, too. The Gospels, Linzey writes, have always urged us to listen to the voiceless, and he quotes biblical scholar Richard Bauckham on the special duty the powerful have to protect those who can't secure rights for themselves.

We need to feel sorrow for the cruelties we inflict on animals; indeed, we need not only to feel that sorrow but also to express it publicly, thereby helping us to change our behavior, to feel greater compassion for all species, including our own.

The issue isn't whether animals go to heaven, therefore, but whether we can give voice to the voiceless.

Animals are the "dumb" innocents "par excellence," wrote Linzey, the ones who cannot speak for themselves, who can suffer horribly at human hands and yet rely totally on humans in order to have any advocates at all. The Gospels, he explained, preach that the "dumb" must be heard, that no matter how deaf humans may be, God "hears the cries of the creatures."

I mentioned to Henry once that as a lifelong urbanite, my new life with animals felt something like a mystery, not because I was saving them, but because they were changing me and teaching me so much, and because I felt so responsible for their welfare.

He said he completely understood.

The power of animals, their animating spirits, the thing that most separates them from us, is this voicelessness. They aren't stupid but mute. We are their spokesmen, their interpreters, their advocates, and their caretakers.

An old tradition holds that at the Last Judgment, the nonhuman creatures of the earth will be called by God to "give evidence" against each human being. The idea pops up in books and stories about the Creation, deemed a myth, but a persistent, imposing, even haunting one: We will be judged by the very creatures so dependent on us.

So I treat, and will continue to treat, my animals—the dogs, cats, sheep, donkeys, chickens, and cows—with that in mind.

They will give evidence. What would I want them to say?

Chapter Eleven

CHASING SUNSETS

By ethical conduct toward all creatures, we enter into
a spiritual relationship with the universe.

—ALBERT SCHWEITZER

THERE IS BOTH AN EERIE BEAUTY AND AN AWFUL BLEAK-
ness to winter in upstate New York, especially after the
holiday brightness. Canadian air piles in; the temperature
plunges; the blackness and cold seem to suck the very life
from the earth.

Everything—everything—is gray, brown, black, or over-
whelmingly white. Sunlight seems to rush past, barely warming the ground.

The animals burrow into barns and corners and hardly
move. The dogs hole up in corners and under beds. The days
are short and utterly bone-chilling.

I'm close to all my dogs, but Izzy is unique. He has a soul
I've never encountered in an animal before. It comes, I think,

from his capacity to see into people, to feel their need, to open deep channels within them.

I don't know if he means to, or how he manages it, but I know that he does it. I've seen him do it time and time again, especially among the dying, people living on the edge of life, people who are suffering.

I'VE NEVER CONSIDERED MYSELF an artist, yet I've always encouraged other people to be artists, sometimes offering valuable encouragement, sometimes pushing them further than they wished to go. That winter, with the help of a smart therapist, I realized that the artist I was urging into the open was me. A creative self seemed to erupt from the photos I'd started taking. And alongside that unfamiliar new self was Izzy, riding with me in the car, lying beside me on the road, my fellow sojourner.

For as long as I can remember, I've been interested in and admired photography—other people's. I doubt I'd taken two dozen pictures of my own to that point, mostly of my daughter's birthday parties or on family vacations, none of them particularly compelling.

But I came across a small digital camera I'd bought on a book tour and stuck in a closet. I began shooting photos of a friend, and one or two of the animals. I'd launched a website by then, so I posted a few.

They were simple, obvious attempts, limited to what was right in front of me—close-ups of faces, snow scenes, the dogs. But these weren't just snapshots.

I'd begun to see the world differently, to experience rebirth, to encounter illumination and to record it, furiously and frantically. I started to notice the beautiful clarity of winter light, the way it outlined barns, bare trees, sheep.

I'd passed dead leaves thousands of times as the dogs and I walked down our woodland path; now I saw how animate they were, rich in emotion, color, and sense of place. I grew conscious of the light dancing everywhere, peeking around corners, framing life. I wanted to capture it, share it.

The stirrings I felt as I noticed this light, the waves of joy and loss, surprised me. I wondered where they were coming from, thinking for a while that it must be something like God whispering to me. Or maybe it was just me, coming alive.

As always, Izzy seemed to sense this stirring and to become part of it. He was wherever I was. I didn't need to ask or train him to do that; he was simply there, almost as much a part of the picture-taking as the camera. I talked to him about light, about what I was seeing, what I hoped to show. He listened, made me feel safe and supported.

I bought a superior (but expensive) camera, a Canon, and then an even better one. I bought a tripod, cleaning kits, lenses. Before long, I was on the phone weekly with B&H Photo in New York, asking about settings, techniques, equipment. I trawled through bookstores for works on photography, for styles I wanted to study, masters to inspire me.

All the while, I took pictures constantly, obsessively, dragging my camera, tripods, and bags everywhere I went. I haunted farms, my own and others, at sunrise, at night, shooting into the sun, around it, behind it, experimenting with focal points, thinking about composition.

This, I knew, was the way I tended to do things—impulsively, obsessively, expensively. But I also knew that I was changing, understanding stuff I hadn't understood before, using abilities I hadn't known how to use. And there, always, was Izzy, observing, standing by, part of the experience.

In the afternoon, when I was finished writing, I would

call Izzy: "Hey, Izzy, boy, let's go chase a sunset." (Rose somehow knew this wasn't her mission, so she went back to the window to watch her sheep.) Izzy dashed out the door and hopped into the backseat of the truck. I loaded up my camera, tripod, and lenses, brought a thermos of hot coffee or tea, turned up the car heater and defrosted the windshield, shivering in the biting cold.

We often drove over the hill to Argyle, around sharp and slick turns, through the bare woods, past staring dairy cows, watching the pale afternoon glow silhouette the old farmhouses. By midafternoon, the sun was dropping fast over the mountains, and I was rushing to catch up with it, chasing a sunset.

Izzy was present in every moment, sitting in the backseat, sitting alongside me, hopping out of the car and along the road.

You wouldn't bring Rose along on a drive like this; she would feel edgy and restless, too confined. Lenore might be too curious and friendly, apt to wander over to visit some creature. Izzy, though, could be with you without ever intruding. He never disturbed a photo, or even moved while I was shooting one; he concentrated on me as intently as I was focused on the camera.

Kinney Road in Argyle, a sloping two-lane blacktop that ran past several dairy farms, was one of the few places nearby with a big, open sky. You could pull over at the bottom of the hill, look up, and see the sun setting against a farmhouse, barns, and silos.

Most days, my teeth were chattering and my fingers—frostbitten several times in winters past—ached and my nose ran. I could feel the wind extracting the heat from my body.

Yet the cold and wet and blasting wind didn't really bother me; I hardly noticed them. Izzy sat watching, his dark eyes fixed on me and what I was photographing. I imagined him saying something like "It's okay, do what you need to do. Take your photos. I'll be here."

By the time we got to Kinney Road and I'd pulled over and climbed out of the car with my new 14mm landscape lens and set up the tripod and mounted the camera, it was growing dark. As is often the case, I had left the house dressed inappropriately for the circumstances, in jeans and walking shoes and a tattered Old Navy sweatshirt.

Cars whizzed by in the dark, sometimes honking because they could barely see me in my dark clothes in the twilight. It *was* unwise to be standing by the roadside that way, but I lost myself, occasionally even wandering out onto the asphalt with my camera, mesmerized by the sinking sun, the farmhouses and silos framed against it. One shouldn't permit most dogs to lie by the road in the gloaming, but I never had to worry about Izzy, who always hopped out with me, found a spot in the shadows far from the passing cars, and never moved.

It was as if some other presence had taken over the process, and I was simply whirling the controls, angling the camera, releasing the shutter. I put the camera up in front of my eyes and walked forward, into the shot. Once, a truck grazed my tripod; another skidded to a screeching halt a few feet from me. I was more lucky than smart, swallowed up by this awakening, these sunsets.

All through the long and bitter winter, Izzy and I chased sunsets through New York State and Vermont, over winding roads and hills, in good weather and bad.

When I was done, the light gone, I looked around, clapped my hand or whistled, called, "Hey, Iz, truck up!" He came around to the passenger side and leaped lightly onto the front seat. I never had to call him twice, nor was he ever distracted by headlights, honks, or the many animals we encountered—deer, coyotes, cows, field mice.

I would turn up the heater, give Izzy a biscuit, sip a bit of tea, head home.

Back on the farm, Rose and Lenore greeted us. We all ventured out for a quick walk, then I fired up the woodstove, took the memory card out of my camera, and put it into my card reader. I watched in the dark, the only light coming from the big computer screen, to see what I had snared and brought home. I was always anxious, sure I had missed the shot, messed up the setting, let in too much light or too little. Sometimes I was right. But I cherished the surge of excitement and satisfaction when even one picture seemed halfway as good as I wanted it to be.

One twilight, when the wind was whipping fiercely and the car's external temperature gauge showed 5 degrees, I looked up Kinney Road and saw a blue and yellow and red sky exploding above the farmhouse—and to my great joy I got the shot. I took, by actual count, more than ten thousand photos that winter, and Izzy was with me for nearly every one.

I never tallied how many miles I logged driving back and forth to Kinney Road, how much gas I used, how many hours I spent there. Izzy never minded. But two or three times a week, Izzy and I climb into the truck and stare up at the barns on Kinney Road, watching the light play across the sky.

———

IZZY BROADENED HIS WORK with people beyond me, especially in our hospice work, which included regular visits to an Alzheimer's/dementia unit in a local nursing home.

In short order, we met Jo, who thought Izzy was her poodle, and Min, who wanted to take him home, and Jen, who asked him to love her, please. Izzy reminded everyone of something—a beloved dog or a cat, a cow or a husband or child. His gentle approach was the key that seemed to unlock parts of people that might otherwise have been impossible to see. He made people smile, laugh, remember.

In subsequent weeks, we entered the building in the same way, punching in codes that unlocked the doors, walking down long hallways, washing hands, wandering into common rooms and gathering places. We encountered people walking quietly, sitting in wheelchairs, gathered around tables or TVs, sometimes sitting alone in their rooms. We made the circuit.

Some people didn't seem to see him, or me, so we passed them by. But others were somehow transformed, as if Izzy had special powers, which to my mind, he did.

The nurses and aides were shocked at first. Then they simply watched as Izzy wafted through Pleasant Valley like a quiet sailboat, spreading good feelings. After a while, staff members started directing Izzy and me to people they thought needed or wanted us. We made many friends, got marriage proposals, danced a few times, joked and flirted.

It was a weekend, always a quieter time, the day we walked past a beautiful woman sitting in a wheelchair, looking somewhat forlornly at a picture hanging on the wall.

I was startled by her beauty. Her white hair was pulled back into a long braid down her back. She couldn't walk by herself. She was distracted, confused, forgetful, yet her blue eyes were radiant, filled with emotion. She was uncomfortable at first, unable to grasp why we were there, what a dog was doing in her room. We must have seemed completely out of context.

But I introduced Izzy to her, and then myself, and she invited us to come sit with her, so we went in. The room was sparsely furnished. A bed, a night table, a dresser.

"Oh, my, what a beautiful dog," she breathed, and you could see her come to life, see how much she loved dogs. She was eager for visitors, it seemed.

She rolled her wheelchair alongside her bed, patted the mattress, and told Izzy to come on up, and he hopped up and curled up next to her, as if he'd been waiting all this time to meet her.

I looked up at the nameplate outside her room. She was Marion and, I learned before long, she was ninety-six, a widowed farm wife. She had an amazing face, very wrinkled but fully alive.

She had to struggle to remember things, and she was losing her sight and her hearing. But Izzy, of course, cared nothing about her deficits. He was happy just to lie calmly on Marion's bed while she stroked his paws and smiled and told him that she loved him and would never hurt him.

A friendship was born. We began visiting her two or three times a week, and the aides told us she would wait by the door, hoping Izzy would be coming. She loved to see him, to touch him, to talk to him about her farm, her children, the other dogs she had known. "But they weren't like you, Izzy," she assured him. "You are the most wonderful dog I ever met."

Marion reached into the deep well of her long life to tell

Izzy what had mattered to her, what she'd loved about her life, even as she sometimes lost track of it. She told him that she forgot things, and couldn't always see, but she never forgot him.

"You will meet my children, Izzy, because they want to meet you," she said to him one afternoon. "Except there is one of my children you will not meet. Hallys. God took her in a hurry, Izzy." She recounted how it was late at night when the state troopers came down the road. She sat up in bed, asking herself, "Who's home?"—because whoever wasn't at home, she realized with awful clarity, was dead.

"And Hallys wasn't home, Izzy. It was Hallys. The troopers said two drunken boys drove across the road in a truck, and she did everything she could to get out of the way, but she couldn't, and she was killed right away, Izzy. She was gone."

There was a long silence in Marion's room. The afternoon light was streaming through the window-blind slats. Outside the door, I could hear the confused cries of some of the patients, the chatter of the staff.

Inside the room, it remained quiet. Izzy lay still, Marion's hands kneading his fur, rubbing his head, holding his paws.

Then I remembered my hospice volunteer training and I leaned forward and said, "Marion, that is so very sad." And she nodded and said, yes, it was, it surely was.

Then she smiled, and told me that her husband's name was Horace, and her blue eyes twinkled. He was "a better man than his name," and so was his father, who was called Eustace. And she turned back to Izzy and promised that she would take care of him and love him forever.

This is what Izzy does. I began bringing cookies and

flowers along on our visits, a quilt my friend Maria made for her, a couple of photos I thought Marion might like. But it was really Izzy that was the best present.

She was confused sometimes, working so hard to remember, to see and hear. Yet she politely asked me questions about my life and my farm. She loved hearing the story of how Izzy had come to me; I told it many times.

She saved bits of doughnuts for him, ignoring my explanation that he didn't need food, wasn't hungry. You don't want a hospice dog to get into the habit of begging for food. But there was no stopping her. She loved Izzy, so she was going to give him something.

At one point, she held out her hand and said, "Here, here is a twenty-dollar bill. Buy Izzy something, please. I just can't get to the store this week." I looked down at her hand, and there was, of course, nothing in it. But I thanked her, and next time I brought her a bag of dog biscuits, so that she could give them to Izzy.

Over time, I learned how to talk with Marion, the angle at which she could best hear and see, the rhythm of my speech that she could most easily follow. I saw that I didn't need to speak so loudly, just clearly.

Hospice advocates "active listening," and I actively listened to Marion. How much of what she told me—about her family, her animals, her life—was accurate I never ascertained. And what did it matter, really? I liked hearing her stories, just as she loved hearing about Izzy, how he ran wild, how untrainable he was at first, how much I treasured him.

We came to know each other. I don't know, perhaps it was a maternal or grandmotherly feeling that she exuded, but I don't think so. It felt more like a friendship, a strong one.

Marion was easy to befriend, uncomplaining and quick to

smile. She spoke in the simple, rich dialect of a farm wife whose life had centered on family, friends, farm chores—and God. "I do believe in Jesus," she told me, matter-of-factly. "Yes, of course."

All the while we spoke, she was stroking Izzy, assuring him that she loved him and would protect him. He was a conduit for all the love in her big heart, and a means by which she was struggling to come to terms with her situation. This is what Izzy does; he's a touchstone for people on passages. This is his soul.

After we spent time with Marion we would make our rounds, see Evelyn cursing at us; Sam calling for his wife, Margaret; Jen asking if we could marry her; Jo asking if Izzy was her dog, the one she lost so many years ago. He could not soothe every resident, but he left a trail of smiles as we walked along.

In late August, the heat and sun abated a bit upstate and when we came to the nursing home, I asked if we could take Marion outside for a wheelchair ride and some time in the open air. She was eager, and the aides helped ready her, got her into her wheelchair with her slippers, a blanket in her lap.

Outside, we sat under a canopy, protected from the sun. Marion was—she told Izzy—having a tough day, a tough time. "I'm just a sick old lady, Izzy. Not good for much. But I won't forget you. I'll never forget you." We talked for a long while about our lives, our farms, our disappointments. She looked at me with her ear cocked forward, so she could hear. She nodded and smiled, seemed to understand.

Then she looked me squarely in the eye, and lowered her voice. "I have to be honest with you, I can't always remember your name," she said. "But I know you and like you. Will you promise me something?"

Yes, I said, if I can.

"Will you promise to take care of Izzy if anything happens to me? If I am gone? Will you promise that he'll never
be mistreated or left to run in the wild? Promise that he will
be loved?"

I looked into those fierce blue eyes, and I answered clearly
and slowly, "I promise, Marion. Izzy will be loved, all the
days of his life."

And she smiled and nodded, relieved.

Chapter Twelve

RUTH AND MAGNUS

A faithful friend is the medicine of life.

—Ecclesiasticus 6:16

IT'S BEEN NEARLY A DECADE SINCE ORSON, A BELOVED, NOW deceased, border collie entered my life, sparked my interest in writing about dogs, and inspired me to buy my own farm. It was also the first time that I gave much thought to dogs and souls.

Early one morning—it seems a long time ago—Orson and I were on the road. He'd seemed restless, circling near the door, a behavior that gets most dog owners moving quickly, even at four a.m. I pulled on my jeans, boots, and a shirt and went outside. That summer night in western Connecticut had been sticky, the cicadas shrill and rhythmic. I moved quietly, not wanting to wake the other participants at this sheep-herding weekend. We veered away from the big house, down a path toward the woods.

In a minute or two, Orson's ruff went up and he began growling; up ahead in the dark I heard a low growl in return. Standing in the woods, half-dressed and tired, I thought none of the possibilities seemed good.

In the moonlight, I could make out a remnant of stone wall along the path, and a red glow from a cigarette, held by a thin, middle-aged woman sitting on the wall. Next to her were a pair of large, glowing yellow eyes, eerie and wolflike.

"Hey," I called, leashing Orson.

"Hello," a voice answered. "Shhh, Magnus."

I put Orson, who was not always delighted to meet strange dogs, in a lie-down.

"Don't worry about Magnus," the woman said. "As long as he can see me, he doesn't much care about anything else." Her voice was striking, deep and sexy, a cross between Garbo and Crawford. She invited me to sit down.

Orson, a wary eye on Magnus, lay down a few feet away. He clearly wanted no trouble.

Nor did Magnus, a large German shepherd, hypnotic in his beauty and stillness. One of those grounded dogs who live quietly and deeply within themselves, he was mostly brown, with streaks of black across his big head. He had presence and power; he was serious, and was to be taken seriously.

This was a one-human dog. He rarely took his eyes off Ruth, except to lie down and doze briefly once in a while. He had no interest in me or Orson or, I came to learn, anyone else.

Ruth also had a quiet dignity; a halo of sadness as well, a sense of being apart. She asked about me, my work, and Orson, but offered very little about herself. Still, she was droll, perceptive, a good listener; the two of us were soon making fun of our herding instructor and some of the other grimly intense students who pursued dog training with the zeal of Crusaders bound for the Holy Land.

"I thought it would be fun," Ruth said. "But I don't see anybody having much fun."

I agreed. Unlike Magnus, Orson was not much of a herding dog—almost three years old when I got him, he had various behavioral troubles. But the truth was, neither of us was taking well to this herding weekend, where people seemed to be queuing up to say that Orson (or I) was facing the wrong way, moving in the wrong direction, doing the wrong thing. I've never taken well to being told what to do, even when my advisers are right; Orson was not much different.

So I was glad to run into Ruth, who had the same authority issues, and Magnus. We quickly became coconspirators and fellow travelers. We abandoned most of the next day's classes and lessons, pleading illness or injury, and took long walks in the woods with our dogs.

It wasn't so easy to talk to Ruth, however comfortable we felt with each other: She went to bed at dusk and got up at two or three a.m. She'd bartered for the herding-camp fee; in exchange for her lessons, she took the sheep out to graze, mucked out the barns, and checked on the water tanks. She didn't seem to take regular meals with the other students; she grabbed vegetables, fruit, or soup on the fly.

The day after that, the session ended. We went our separate ways, but not before exchanging phone numbers and email addresses.

I VISITED RUTH at her farm in western New York State a few months later. Hers was a classically decaying dairy farm—the sprawling old white farmhouse with peeling paint, the giant faded-red barns for cows and hay, the moldering piles of hay and manure.

We'd communicated regularly since our first meeting, and she'd suggested that I bring Orson and come to see her.

I wasn't sure what, or whom, I'd find there. Ruth had mentioned a husband in one of her emails—the first I had heard of one—but I gathered that he was not living on the farm. I wasn't sure I'd ever exactly find out; Ruth didn't like saying too much about herself.

I pulled into the big drive around her farm in late afternoon. She was sitting on the front porch, waiting for me, Magnus stretched out by her feet.

She was probably in her late fifties, a wiry woman with deep eyes in a lined face, a chain-smoker who consumed each cigarette to the nub and almost immediately lit another.

She brought out a pitcher of iced tea; we sat in Adirondack chairs and watched the sun lower and a few deer emerge from the dusk.

I tossed Magnus a biscuit, but he ignored it, until Ruth nodded; then he scarfed it down. I had more in my pocket, but he just put his big beautiful head down on his paws and closed his eyes.

I could see why Ruth and her mysteriously absent husband had picked this spot. I didn't have my own farm yet; perhaps the idea grew on me during visits to Ruth's.

She had an unusual story: She'd grown up on a Nebraska farm, moved to New York for college, then went on to do graduate study in philosophy at Columbia in the early 1970s. She had hoped to teach and write.

But during an affair with another grad student, she became pregnant and, though single, decided to have the child.

Desperate for tuition money, working several jobs, she signed up for a campus job fair. A Justice Department recruiter was interested in her; the DEA, it turned out, was looking for agents, especially those who could work undercover. Pregnant women were effective and much in demand, the recruiter explained, because they aroused little suspicion among drug dealers.

Ruth took to this strange new career more than she might have imagined. She liked the challenging, high-risk nature of the job; she liked the security of a regular paycheck.

It had its less pleasant moments, too. Since I knew her only in the context of dogs, sheepherding, and our soon to be parallel experience of owning a farm and living with animals, it was easy to forget how dramatic her previous life had been. She'd been chased, beaten, shot at twice, stabbed, and "scared out of my wits" a dozen times.

Even after her son, Raphael, was born, she sometimes stuffed a pillow under her sweater so that she could keep working undercover as a pregnant woman. She perfected various other disguises, too—a homeless person, a bus driver, a junkie.

But once she had tasted that life, she told me on the single occasion she discussed her career in law enforcement, she couldn't go back to academia or business. "Life would have seemed too dull."

Somewhere during these years, she married John, a U.S. customs agent. In twenty-five years together, they lived up and down the East Coast, working hard, raising Rafe, buoyed by the same dream: One day they'd own a farm.

In the late nineties, after distinguished careers, they both retired. Along with her trophies and citations, Ruth kept her badge and her 9mm pistol; she was still called in for undercover jobs from time to time. She and John found their farm, this 140-acre haven a couple of hours south and west of Buffalo, with a pre–Civil War farmhouse, plenty of pasture, rolling hills, a stream, and patches of dense woods.

They acquired sheep, goats, and a couple of horses. They built gardens and fences, painted buildings and barns, found a tenant farmer to plant corn and alfalfa, and spent a fortune on new and improved water systems.

"We were insanely happy," she said. "This was our lifelong dream, and we'd done it." The work was brutal, the hours long, and they had a lot to learn, much of it from their mistakes. But they loved rural life, even the chores and challenges. They sold livestock and cheese.

Both of their work lives had been tense and harried—lots of time away from home, lots of stress—so it was especially sweet for John and Ruth to finally have a peaceful place, common interests, and the time to share them. They'd never had the luxury of that kind of time before.

She was driving to town one afternoon when she saw a big brown-and-black dog lying by the roadside, his legs splayed and bloodied, but his chest still rising and falling. The nearest vet's office was nearly thirty miles away, but she managed to get the dog into the truck and drive there, exceeding the speed limit the entire way. Magnus had been hit and left to die, the vet said. It cost a thousand dollars or more and took months of rehab, but Magnus recovered, thanks to good work by the vet and loving care from Ruth. By the time we met, apart from a barely noticeable limp, the dog showed no outward signs of his trauma.

"Looking back," Ruth told me now as we sat on the porch and she filled in some of the blanks, "I see that Magnus came to be with me, to prepare me for what would happen. I helped him recover, and he understood that one day he'd do the same for me."

Ruth never struck me as religious, but she had a mystical streak, one Magnus somehow triggered. And who could say—perhaps she was right.

What happened was that her son, Raphael, by then a college student in Philadelphia, sustained grave injuries in a car crash on his way back to school after winter break. He spent weeks in a hospital on life support before Ruth could agree to let him die.

John, always a heavy drinker, sank into alcoholism, and his physical and mental condition deteriorated so rapidly that a year later he needed a nursing home. Ruth found a good facility a half day's drive from their farm. He spent a year there, and then John, too, was dead.

The medical bills from Raphael's, and then John's, deaths were staggering, and Ruth's losses paralyzing. The farm, so energizing just a short time earlier, began to collapse. Fences broke, water froze, the barn roof collapsed, animals got sick, the fields flooded. A foal died. Coyotes killed four of her sheep.

"If I were religious," Ruth told me, "I would've thought that God was punishing me, striking me down. But I couldn't say for what."

The farm, first a fantasy, then a reality, then a grim burden, was consuming her, she said. It helped that she could barter services with other women living nearby. "There were a lot of single women with a lot of land around," she found. They painted one another's houses, fixed fences, helped with animal care, borrowed tractors for mowing and brush-hogging.

They helped Ruth keep her farm going, but they couldn't

do much for her mental health. "I completely lost the ability to socialize, to make small talk and chitchat," she told me. "I couldn't bear the news, or politics, or TV. I shed my friends. I couldn't handle everybody asking me how I was all the time."

Probably the only thing that helped her endure was Magnus, by her side in the fields, on walks, during chores, in the truck, alongside the sofa, at the foot of the bed. He went to the cemetery with her. "He was more than my shadow," Ruth said. "He fused with me. He was there for everything, every part of it."

Sitting on the porch, I felt honored that she'd asked me and Orson to visit, and afraid for her, too. How long could she keep this longed-for enterprise going by herself? And how much could she rely on a dog, even one this faithful, for sustenance?

Loneliness is so painful a condition that it's used as torture. They call it solitary confinement, and its purpose is to break people. Humans are innately social, and our social systems are constructed so that we can do few things without interacting with others. Life on my farm is quiet, with few people around much of the time, but to do almost anything—buy hay, get animals inoculated, shop for groceries, fill a gas tank—I have to encounter other people. This is probably fortunate.

Because however much I love the farm and my life here, sometimes, when it's dark or cold or the wind is howling outside, when it's so still that I suddenly can detect the beating of my own heart, I miss my wife and my daughter. I remember times in life when I've been even more alone, and not by choice. The pain and sadness can feel overwhelming. How much harder, unimaginably harder, to be unable to pick up a phone and hear their voices.

At these times, I look around me, and always—always—see a dog nearby. Rose is watching from across the room, or Izzy is looking into my eyes, or Lenore has curled up next to me. They are offering themselves to me, and the communication between us becomes almost palpable. *You are not alone,* they seem to be saying. And I think, Well, I'm *not* alone, at least not as alone as I felt.

Having Izzy's head on my knee is not the same as sharing the daily news of life with someone I love, not as meaningful as taking care of a young child. Those things can't be replaced. Maybe, in a more perfect world, time could stop, there would be no more pain, and the things I cherish would always be there. But time moves forward, we grow older, lives take unpredictable turns. Still, better Izzy than no one. Much better. And better Magnus than the blackness of Ruth's memories. No wonder we love our animals so much, owe them so much, and wish so fervently that they will be with us always. The soul of a dog is its faithfulness, its friendship, its comfort.

THE SUN WAS COMING UP, and Ruth and I were walking in the pasture behind her farmhouse. She'd made a wonderful breakfast of fresh coffee and home-baked corn muffins and local eggs. Magnus loped around her flock of sheep and gathered them into the barn, where Ruth was distributing grain in feed troughs to pregnant ewes.

Orson walked happily alongside us, mostly ignoring the sheep, staying out of Magnus's way. We had slept well in a guest cabin by the side of house, and it was pleasant to keep

Ruth company as she fed the horses and goats and checked the fences.

Then we headed back into her roomy old kitchen, circa 1956, complete with fluorescent lighting and linoleum floors, for more coffee. In Ruth's house, comfortable and unpretentious, you could almost see generations of farm families chowing down at the kitchen table before hitting the tractors and the fields. That sense of hard work spanning a century or two was what she loved about the farm. That and her nearly silent, but indispensable, companion.

"What can I say?" she said later, taking a drag on her Camel. "Magnus was all I could really count on, and he came through. I'm probably out of my mind, but I believe he was guiding me."

After the weekend I'd met her, she'd dropped the herding lessons. She just went out with the dog every day, and the two of them had figured out how to operate. I'd soon take the same approach with Rose when I bought my own farm, not caring precisely which way her butt was pointing, only that she brought the sheep when I asked her to, the way Magnus did. There was something beautiful, I told Ruth, about just working it out on your own farm with your own dog, even if that sort of home-schooling drove some purists crazy.

Ruth wasn't only talking about herding, though. She was used to being alone, she said, and had never needed a lot of people, yet she'd never been this alone. The shock, the loss, the grief, it was hard even for a strong person to bear. But she'd be out walking in the fields sometimes, she confided, and she'd hear a message. "Hang on," someone or something would tell her. "Hang on." And there was nobody there but Magnus.

She hung on. When loneliness got unbearable, she said,

Magnus came over to lick her hand, hop up on the sofa, lie next to her in bed. His constancy never wavered. "You couldn't distract him away from me," Ruth said. Aside from the sheep, "he didn't care about other dogs or animals or people. He has a mission, and his mission is my survival."

We spoke once or twice a week, recommended books we thought the other would like, sent email. She couldn't come to visit me—couldn't handle the drive, she said. So, I visited her on her farm, perhaps twice a year, and we would talk through the afternoon, then resume early in the morning. We herded sheep together, took walks, shared chores. I loved visiting her peaceful retreat, learned skills I would soon come to need, admired the life she'd struggled to build and was fighting to keep. There was beauty and freedom in her loneliness.

Ruth eventually came to Bedlam Farm a couple of times. She couldn't leave her place for long, since she had to ask neighbors to watch the animals, so she stayed for only a night.

She would arrive in the afternoon. We would walk around the farm or through the woods, herd the sheep together, have something to eat. Then she would disappear into the guest room, slipping out every half hour or so to smoke. I told her she was welcome to smoke indoors; she said thanks and ignored me. All during her visits, I was conscious of red lights glowing here and there around the farm at night, with Magnus's eyes often glowing alongside. Then, without a word, she would vanish, out of sight for the night.

In the morning, no matter how early I got up, she and Magnus were already out. Ruth had ferocious feelings about paying her own way, carrying her own freight, so by dawn any dishes left in the sink were done and there was a pot of fresh coffee and muffins just out of the oven. When I walked outside, I found the animals already fed, the water troughs filled, the chickens happily picking at muffin crumbs.   ·

Magnus was as happy to herd my sheep as his own, but apart from that, he paid scant attention to my animals, or to the other dogs. He watched Ruth, his eyes following her as she worked. Orson he ignored, as usual.

People gave him a wide berth, not because he behaved aggressively but because they found him intimidating. People are afraid of big dogs with big teeth. And he certainly did give the impression—though I don't know if it was true—that anyone who tried to mess with Ruth would get torn to pieces.

It didn't really matter what he would do so much as what people thought he might, Ruth pointed out. Even on her isolated farm, she felt safe with Magnus.

While I worked, Ruth and Magnus disappeared, out with the sheep, walking in the woods, sitting in the meadow. When I'd had enough time staring at the computer, they materialized. We sat by the woodstove with mugs of coffee in the winter, Magnus at her feet, Orson or Rose at mine; if it was summer, we were all out on the front porch.

Because Ruth kept such odd hours, and because she was so extraordinarily independent and helpful, her visits always felt too short.

You could get only so close to Ruth, anyway. Though we talked frequently, the shroud of aloneness that enveloped her never fully dissipated. I couldn't claim to know what she was thinking or feeling, not because she was devious or dishonest, but because her feelings ran so deep. I suppose she confined them to the journal she kept. She wrote poetry, too, but I never saw it.

When we first met, Ruth seemed very grounded to me,

strong and clear-headed. As time went on, she seemed less so. She sounded more uncertain.

She looked different, too.

When she visited one fall, I noticed that a couple of teeth were missing from the side of her mouth. They'd had to be removed, she explained, but she didn't have the money to replace them yet. Her skin looked sallow, the lines in her face deeper. She reeked of tobacco.

The farm was overwhelming her, she said; so were her debts. She was running out of ideas. She and her neighbor women were wearing one another out, trying to keep their farms going, and Ruth didn't want to be taking advantage of them. "I've tried everything," she said as we walked with our dogs. "Different crops, different sheep. I don't have the money. I don't have the strength." She was thinking of trading the farm she and John had bought for a much smaller one, just thirty acres, one town over.

By now, Ruth was coughing a lot. She'd given up drinking when John died—she used to love whiskey—but I doubted she'd ever stop smoking. She'd lost weight. I could almost imagine her vanishing into the darkness.

She'd become just about entirely nocturnal, I told her, like a vampire. She smiled. "I think I might like living like a vampire," she said.

This was a different friend. Perhaps she'd been forced to absorb too many blows. "I'm grateful Magnus came to me," she said on our walk. By now, Orson was gone; we were walking with Izzy, Rose, and Pearl. "Magnus is my dark-time dog. That's why he's here, to see me to the other side."

I was alarmed. Did Ruth mean that Magnus was going to guide her out of this world? That she was going to die? Or wanted to? No, she said, she meant that the dog was guiding her as she shifted from one sort of life to another, "from a place of expectations, to none." She wanted to let go of grief. She'd accepted that she'd never have a child again. She'd given up on the notion of finding another partner; she was preparing to let go of her farm. The "other side" was a place where she didn't feel the lack of such things.

I sputtered about hope, about still being young enough for change, about the unpredictable nature of life.

She just sounded tired. "You're still on this side," she said, "so you can't understand. You have your wife, your daughter, your friends, your work. I'm losing all of that, and I don't know if I'll ever get them back, or if I even want to. Magnus will help me across to a different part of life. I do expect him to be there; he's always there."

I wasn't sure what to make of it, to be honest. The attachment between the two of them was indeed profound. Always the faithful friend, Magnus wasn't anxious, distracted, needy, or even playful. For years, he'd simply lived to be with Ruth, to accompany her through her increasingly traumatic life. But the way she spoke of him now, like Charon on the river Styx, was disturbing.

Ruth became difficult to reach after that autumn visit. Her emails and phone calls came less regularly. When we finally connected, she reported that she had in fact swapped properties with a farmer a few miles away, which made things easier, although she missed her old place. In the process, she'd sold off the horses and goats and most of the sheep, keeping just a few for Magnus's sake. She could no longer afford to care for many animals, she said, "and if I can't care for them well, I shouldn't have them."

Then, for a couple of months, nothing.

ONE DAY a card arrived: "Dearest Jon, I'm writing to say goodbye. I can't make it on a farm, and my sister in Oregon is dying of cancer. I am going out to help her. She doesn't have long, and I can be of some use there for the time she does have. I've put the farm up for sale and left things to a broker.

"I'm sorry not to be more in touch, but I value you very much, treasure our times together and love you and wish you well."

When I tried to call I found that the number had been disconnected. My emails started bouncing back, too.

I eventually discovered the number of her sister, outside Portland. A man answered when I called—Ruth's uncle, he said—and told me the sister had died two weeks earlier. Ruth's presence had been "a great blessing" at the end. After the memorial service—more loss—she'd left, saying she was going to travel for a bit, and that she'd let the family know when she landed. She hadn't left any address, no way to stay in touch.

Was there a dog with her? I asked.

Oh yes, said the man. Big and somewhat intimidating, but very devoted. "I don't think I ever saw him leave her side."

I missed Ruth, our herding together, our talks and walks. I could never reconcile her love of rural life with her gun-toting undercover past, another reminder not to make assumptions about people. And I couldn't imagine how she'd kept going as long as she did, given all that had befallen her. A good friend—attentive, sympathetic, funny—she'd handled the tragedy and disappointment that engulfed her bravely, without complaint or self-pity. But the demands of even a stripped-down life had become too much.

In the realm of different expectations where she and Magnus were headed she might feel freer. I hoped so. I believed Ruth wanted to be alone with her grief, to live simply and peacefully with Magnus, her companion and guardian.

It wasn't what she'd wanted when she and John dreamed about their farm, or when she and Rafe had talked about his future. But maybe it was what made sense to her now.

I thought about what James Serpell, who writes about the human-animal bond and the role animals play in our lives, said in his book *In the Company of Animals*.

"Pets complement and augment human relationships," he wrote. "They add a new and unique dimension to human social life and, thereby, help to buffer effects of loneliness and social isolation. Perhaps, in the best of all possible worlds, it would be preferable if humans satisfied all their social and affiliative needs with each other. The world would no doubt be a happier and saner place as a result."

But, he added, until that happier day comes, "we can do a great deal worse than seek the partial fulfillment of these needs in the company of animals."

Often, as I walk in the woods with my dogs, I wonder where Ruth has settled, how she is faring, whether she is peaceful, or even happy. It hurts a bit that she left me behind, that our friendship has become one of those expectations she felt she had to jettison.

We'd shared some powerful things—a love of dogs and farms, a mutual sense of growing together, along with a mutual sense of outsiderness. We'd decided to live outside the mainstream. We both found ourselves a little ridiculous, and enjoyed noticing how.

Now, thinking of animals and souls, it was impossible not to picture Magnus, whose fidelity had shored Ruth up, who'd stepped in to provide what humans couldn't give her any longer.

It's possible for people who suffer such losses to recover, to find new people to love. But Ruth seemed to have decided that this was never going to happen. Perhaps she couldn't bear to try, to risk it all over again. Perhaps she was simply too weary, after seeing so much of her life collapse so quickly and tragically.

It's in the nature of friendship, I guess, to never give up on one's friends, to offer sympathy and encouragement and concern—perhaps things Ruth didn't need or want. It's in human nature to try to lift each other up, even those who don't wish to be lifted.

Magnus would never push Ruth to hang on to her farm, as I had, or reassure her that she could meet other people, as I did, or tell her how sorry he was about what she'd suffered. He wouldn't crack jokes to make her laugh, or ship books to distract her.

I *meant well,* as friends do. But dogs *do good,* letting their humans live, rather than telling them how. I think I understand better what Ruth meant when she talked about Magnus's guiding her to another sphere—not death, but a different kind of life, where she could find peace by ceasing to have to strive.

As Serpell has written, she could do a great deal worse than seeking out the company of her remarkable dog. I know he's sitting by her side somewhere, offering himself to her as a companion on her haunting journey.

I don't see how she could have done better.

THE MYSTERY OF THINGS

Perhaps that is part of the animals' role among us,
to awaken humility, to turn our minds back
to the mystery of things, and open our hearts
to that most impractical of hopes in which
all creation speaks as one.

—MATTHEW SCULLY, *Dominion: The Power of Man,*
the Suffering of Animals, and the Call to Mercy

THE WEATHER STATION ON MY KITCHEN RADIO IS FILLED with apocalyptic warnings: frigid cold descending from Canada tonight, heavy sleet, shrieking winds, a windchill of 25 below zero.

This news grabs my attention, transforms the day. I confer hurriedly with Annie. I call the large-animal vet, the local farm supply store, and several neighboring farmers to see if they've heard the forecast, to plot strategy, and make sure the animals are cared for. I call a friend to see what he's heard (his source in the town's highway department says it's going to be bad).

I start hauling firewood indoors, near the stoves. The furnace won't keep this drafty old farmhouse warm in bitter cold and high winds, so I need to keep the wood dry.

I pull my car and truck into the barn, make sure there's enough sand for the driveways and walkways. I rush to the Bedlam Corners Variety Store for milk and bread. Annie and I haul pots and buckets of hot water out to the barnyard water valves, which are already frozen.

I push back the mild panic I feel. There's often trouble in extreme weather, but we always get through it. There is help if I need it.

The necessities for people are simple, cheap, and readily available. But the animals are another story. When I hear dire weather reports, I become tense, anxious, distracted. I can't relax until I've prepared for their care, and even then I'm likely to have a long, restless night thinking of them out in the bitter winds, listening for cries of distress, going out to check on them.

I know they are hardy and resilient, but they can suffer in this kind of weather, even die. And that's not acceptable. I can't let an animal of mine freeze in a winter storm.

This is a weight that people with animals bear. I know what locals mean when they say they get tired of the responsibilities and look forward to being free of the worry. It would be nice, I think, to just see a movie tonight and get some good pizza, things abundant in New Jersey but not in my little upstate hamlet.

By nightfall, which comes awfully early this time of year, I'd better have what I need, and the animals had better have what they need.

I've been at this for more than five years now, and I've learned a lot, but it never seems easy. I always feel vulnerable to that one stiff gust of wind, one night of bitter cold, one short-circuited wire corroded by ice and water.

Car batteries die in this kind of cold; driveways and roads can become impassable; windshield wipers stick, and windshield-washer fluid freezes. It's no fun having a farm on such a night.

Annie and I ponder once more whether to bring the cows into the barn to spare them from the punishing winds, or to leave them to huddle against a big round hay bale. It's healthier for them outside, I know, if they can be protected from the wind. Elvis doesn't fit easily into a barn: He's likely to butt out windows with his head or bang into beams. Bringing him inside, I've come to see, is something *I* need, not something *he* needs.

Still, uneasy, I call the large-animal vet. Sarah laughs at me. I call her nearly every time there's a blizzard or a torrential downpour. She always tells me the same thing, and I always need to hear it. As long as they have some shelter, keep the cows outside, she says. Concrete-floored barns are not warm. If they can get out of the wind—and they can—they will do fine.

Still, Annie and I tote out grain, to give them energy, and second-cut hay, which is more nutritious (and expensive) than the first-cut they usually get. We make sure the water troughs are full and the deicers working. We know from past experience that this kind of cold alters matter. Valves freeze, hoses crack, pipes burst.

We plug in the heated water bucket for the chickens, and put out three days' worth of feed. We turn on a heatlamp so that aging Winston and his hens will have extra warmth. We fill the bird feeders, too.

We build a hay igloo in the loft for Mother and put out a tin of dried cat food, which won't freeze.

We prepare to bring the donkeys inside for the night, though. They're hardy, but might be tempted to stay out to guard the sheep and could stumble on an icy hillside. Just a few weeks earlier, Jeannette slipped and fell; struggling to right herself, she clambered to her feet only when Rose nipped her in the butt, urging her up.

So we clean out the barn's middle room, spread straw for bedding, tape up any wires and remove sharp objects (donkeys chew things). We put out grain and hay, get another huge heated water bucket and plug it in.

Next, we haul out the sand, scattering it inside the pasture gate and around the water feeder for the animals, and the salt for the places where people walk.

The sheep will be fine in the pole barn, we figure, protected on three sides from the wind and cold, or up in the pasture, where they usually clump. But they'll need energy, so Annie hauls extra hay into the pole-barn feeders so the sheep won't have to brave an icy slope down to the big feeder by the barn. And she strews straw for warmer bedding. We worry about the five-month-old lambs; they have fleece, but not as much as their mothers.

I take the three dogs down to the meadow across the road and toss slingshot rubber balls for them. They need this exercise now, since they won't be going out much for the next day or so. They tear back and forth across the big, windswept field, happy even though the thermometer says 2 degrees. Rose chases the ball; Izzy chases Rose; Lenore tries unsuccessfully to keep up with both of them. Border collie and Lab fun. After twenty minutes, by which point my fingers will barely move, the dogs' tongues are out, a signal that we can stop.

Human bodies are vulnerable, too: I've had two bouts of frostbite, and now, my circulation impaired, I can't stay outside long in such temperatures; my fingers will ache painfully even after I'm inside. Back in the farmhouse, I lay out extra sweaters, wool caps, thermal boots. In winter, I make frequent use of a paraffin-bath gizmo, dipping my hands in melted wax to keep them warm and keep the blood moving. Otherwise I hurt and, worse, I can't work.

By noon, we're all already exhausted, but we're ready. We've thawed out the valves, dragged out the hay, filled the grain buckets, stacked the firewood, laid out the straw bedding. The water troughs are full. I've checked the furnace to be sure there's oil enough in the tank, and carried in two nights' firewood.

In strong winds, with so many trees and limbs still ice-covered from the previous storm a few days ago, the likelihood of losing power is high, so I place candles and flashlights at strategic points around the house.

In late afternoon, Annie and I make a final check. The chickens have instinctively retreated early to their roosts, warmed by the heatlamp. I worry about Winston, who clearly is slowing down.

No one can tell me that animals don't have their own brand of weather forecasting. Never is it more evident than before a storm, as the chickens, slipping into their vegetative state, remind me. It's not supposed to get brutal for hours yet, but they're already hunkered down, still and waiting.

The others have their own specific rituals. When the weather gets ugly, my sheep usually climb to the highest point in the pasture, for reasons unclear to me or anyone else.

They have other options. They can go into the big barn—I usually leave the sliding door ajar on nasty nights. They could easily gather in the pole barn, the most logical place for shelter and food. But they almost always head for the top of the hill.

I've watched as they walk up slowly, almost solemnly, a trek that can take nearly an hour, with its own eerie rhythms. Two or three ewes move forward, then stop; three or four more amble a few steps farther, then stop. Eventually, they circle tightly, the lambs in the middle, each sheep tucked against two or three others, with virtually no space between them. Then they don't move, sometimes for hours, sometimes for a day or two.

In winter, I often look up to see the whole clump blanketed with snow, waiting out the storm. And as the uphill migration begins, that's what seems likely tonight.

The donkeys have commandeered the pole barn, peering out. They're almost always ready to skitter over to the gate for a cookie, but this afternoon, as the temperature drops and the skies turn a dark metal gray, they stare as I wave carrots and cookies, and refuse to come out.

The cows are perhaps the most indifferent. You get the sense that as long as they have hay and water, nothing much can trouble them, certainly not something as fleeting as snow. I've never seen them visibly uncomfortable, except when the vicious flies of summer descend.

On the eve of this storm, they mostly follow their normal routines, except that Elvis and Luna are under the feeder roof, nestled against round bales of hay. Harold is nearby, gnawing on a tree.

Rose is very busy, rushing up to the pole barn to bark at Lulu, taking a run at Mother, the barn cat, when she ventures out (Mother gives her a contemptuous stare from atop a fencepost), dashing up to check on sheep, then back to me.

Perhaps she's picked up a sense of urgency from Annie and me, but she keeps repeating this ritual, running from one spot to the next. Izzy plops down next to me wherever I am.

So does Lenore. Her work is love—loving me, loving everybody, and I like it; it nourishes me.

As prepared as we can be, I take the dogs inside and they begin to settle, finding their own quiet corners in advance of the storm.

The fired-up stoves are already roaring.

THERE'S A PART of each animal on my farm that I don't understand, another dimension.

I can't fathom how Rose grasps the life of the farm so intuitively, seeming to recognize what needs to be done; I puzzle over whether the judgments she makes are based on instinct or reason.

Does Elvis actually understand how humans work, or is he just so appealing and good-natured a creature that we see in him what we wish?

I can't figure out how Mother can be purring softly in my lap one minute, and pulling the head off a songbird the next. Which is her real soul?

Why does Lenore hang out with sheep? Was she born with this capacity for affection? Did her mother lavish more attention on her than on her littermates? Or did I need her to be this way, and encourage her to make this her work?

I can't say that Izzy chose to be my dog, as my vet thinks. Maybe he was simply waiting to be anybody's dog, and I just happened along. Either way, it's hard to express just how instinctively and completely he's entered my life.

I can't say why Winston appeared to like Orson, or at least sought out his company, when he's shown no interest in any other dog since. Or why Henrietta the hen had so much personality, while the other hens seem so generic.

And that spirituality the donkeys exude—is it real? Does it

come from thousands of years of standing by to serve, and observe, humans? If they were as small as dogs, I think they'd probably end up sleeping in our beds, too.

I can attempt explanations, but in the end I have to admit how much of their behavior and motives is unknowable. Perhaps that's part of their appeal.

I HAVE DINNER, listen to my kitchen weather radio, try to read, call friends while I still have phone service. By ten p.m. the storm is in full swing. The ice and sleet spatter audibly against the living room's tall old windows, and the winds shriek around the corners. The outside thermometer that hangs by the kitchen window says minus 18. How many storms, I wonder, has this house seen since the Civil War?

I always make a final check on the animals in weather like this, and this time, I feel an acute sense of being very alone. Annie can no longer get her truck out of her driveway, she calls to tell me. If I had some crisis, my farmer friends would come, even if it meant riding over on their John Deeres, but they will have their own problems. And any official emergency crew—sheriff's department, ambulance corps, volunteer firefighters—will have more critical tasks.

So I need to take care. It's easy to slip, fall, be butted or kicked, and in such weather it could be a while before anybody noticed I was outside on my ass, risking hypothermia. I usually call somebody when I go out on a tough night, with a request to send help if I don't call again in an hour. Tonight, I call two.

I bundle up with thermal gloves, winter boots, a heavy parka with a horse comb in one pocket. I take a cell phone, even though it probably won't work up in the pasture, and a huge flashlight, and tuck a towel into the waistband of my jeans. Instead of walking through the pasture gate, Rose and I use a smaller gate behind the house.

It's as brutal as expected: the wind blowing in great gusts, driving needles of ice and snow horizontally into my face. Rose is instantly covered, and I see ice balls beginning to collect on her feet, though she's gone just a short distance. My eyes tear, my toes and fingers and ears hurt.

Out in the pasture, Rose pauses, nearly blown backward by the wind. I shine my light, barely able to see fifty feet ahead. But when the winds shifts, or there's a small break in the snow, I can see pairs of eyes up the hill, illuminated by the beam. That would be the sheep in their tight, snowy cluster. Rose looks up at the flock, but she doesn't run up to bother them. She always knows when to work and when to leave things alone.

We trundle about a hundred yards to the pole barn, where the donkeys are huddled in a corner. Their eyelids and nostrils are ringed with icicles. We seem all alone up here, as if the rest of the world has receded, preoccupied with its own troubles.

The donkeys and I have been through this before. I take out the comb and remove the frozen ice from their ears and manes, wipe the mucus from their nostrils. Very carefully, with a gloved hand, I push the ice from their eyelashes. They hold up their heads for me, somehow (but how?) understanding that I won't hurt them, that this is not medicine or a shot. It almost seems as if they like it. I do.

Carefully inching back down the hill, I look around for Mother, but there's no sign of her. In storms, she disappears, into some secret spot. Any of my dogs, except perhaps for Rose, would be yowling to come inside the house on a night like this, but Mother won't come in, not even if I leave the cellar door open a crack.

I walk over to the paddock to look down at the cows, all gathered around the feeder, eating hay. Cows have their priorities in order.

It takes us a good while to get back to the house. The ground is terribly slippery, the ice being covered by a thickening layer of blowing snow, so even walking is tricky.

Inside, I unwrap myself, greet Izzy and Lenore, take out a towel for the intrepid Rose, covered in ice, with snowballs clinging to her fur. I put on some water for tea, pour a shot of scotch from my bottle of Glenlivet, collapse into a chair by the big woodstove. I rarely drink alcohol these days, but in a storm, with a fire going, it's nice to take a sip.

I put my feet up on the table, sit on one hand, then the other to thaw my fingers, and call my friends to give the all clear.

Thawing on the rug beside me, Rose looks tired and drifts off to sleep. Izzy hops up onto the sofa next to me; Lenore lumbers over, licks my hand furiously, then plops back onto her dog bed.

I'm enveloped by loving dogs on this awful night. They're fortunate to be inside, curled up around the stove. My animals outside are in for a long and different kind of night.

This night, I think, has presented a chance to be compassionate and responsible, to be humbled both by animals' stamina and the ferocity, sometimes, of their environment.

I'm satisfied that I've done everything I can do—until Rose growls and rushes to the window, apparently alarmed. So I suit up again, more wearily, and as we head out I grab a Snickers bar; a treat can't hurt Elvis on a night like this. This time the thermometer reads minus 20.

What's triggered Rose's protectiveness?

Rose has a map in her head of how the farm ought to

be—I have no such internal guide—and when something is amiss, a sound, a cry, a strange movement, she reacts, and thus alerts me. This has happened so often that I almost take it for granted. It is simply what she does, and when I go to sleep, I am relatively secure in the knowledge that if something is wrong, Rose will sense it and sound the alarm.

Half-afraid of what I'll find—and forgetting to let anyone know I've ventured outside again in frostbite weather—I climb up to the gate and sweep the pasture with my torch-light. I see movement, and peer through the snow. Jesus and Fanny are playing, chasing each other around and around the pole barn as the wind whips past them and blasts drifts of snow across the pasture.

Jesus tears across the field and vanishes behind a pine tree. Jeannette peers out of the pole barn, disapprovingly, but doesn't intervene as Fanny goes tearing after him. The two often play this game, but why are they feeling playful on a night this miserable? It's yet another tutorial in things I don't know.

Rose and I make our way into the big barn, where the chickens are asleep. Mother pops up on a gate to say a purring hello; she's quite dry, so she's probably stayed nestled upstairs in the hayloft.

Opening the gate to the paddock, admitting an inferno of wind-driven ice, I see Elvis, still chowing down at the feeder. He spots me and, with a strange sound of greeting, comes ambling over, perhaps to see if I've brought anything tasty.

Between Elvis and me lies my fancy new grain feeder, a three-by-six contraption of heavy steel that set me back $500. Its several compartments allow each animal to eat without butting heads with the others, or strewing the grain all over the ground.

Elvis, breaking into a trot, sails right into the new feeder, and it crumples like a sheet of paper. He keeps walking and mashes the rest of it into scrap metal without even seeming to notice that it's there.

He comes up to the fence, and I give him his Snickers and brush a cap of snow off the top of his head. I pat him, tell him I'm sorry for the long, cold night he will endure, contemplate the mangled cow feeder—so much for that agricultural innovation. Then I leave Godzilla and go back with Rose through the barn and into the house.

I have to remember, I tell myself, that this night is not the same for them as it is for me. They need food and water and the option of shelter, but they live in the now. They may feel some discomfort, but weather is part of their lives, another cycle in their own rituals, instincts, and traditions.

These nights remind me of the mystery of things. The Trappist monk and author Thomas Merton, of whom I'm a faithful reader, called these moments "journeys of the soul." I've come to believe that our encounters with certain animals can, at times, mark journeys of the soul; they may even accompany us on them.

On such nights, I often feel that my animals reveal their souls. The storm, which has us humans running around like panicked mice, means little to them. They may respond with calm acceptance, with playfulness, with a chocolate craving. It's never more clear that they're not like us, hunkering down in our heated houses, watching the weather nervously to try to anticipate what the animals seem to already know. Only the dogs, those adept social parasites, will spend the night as I do, indoors, dry and warm.

What animals know or think or want falls into that gray zone amid what religion preaches, what science shows, and what we see with our own eyes and believe. Mystery may be the greatest gift my animals provide: It keeps me humble; it evokes the potential of life. It's enthralling sometimes to wonder and not to know, to be reminded of the profoundly limited knowledge of arrogant and destructive human beings.

THE STORM LINGERED for most of two days, shifting from snow and gusting winds to freezing rain. Power outages struck all around me, but to my surprise the farm was spared, even as tree limbs were coated with ice and the roads grew treacherous.

The dogs—Izzy and Rose in particular—cut their pads running on the ice, leading to some bleeding. At one time this would have seemed a veterinary medical crisis; now it merely precipitated a two-minute drill. I already had the antibiotic cream, the gauze, the self-adhesive bandages it took Rose a good half hour to unravel.

The animals did seem a bit happier than usual to see Annie and me the third morning. The donkeys brayed more insistently than they typically do, waiting at the gate for their cookies; the chickens came rushing over for the Cheerios and birdseed I scattered as a restorative.

Elvis looked positively ebullient when I came out with my Snickers, lumbering over for his daily treat, then lingering, head down, for some neck scratching.

But the sheep were their normal selves; though swathed in ice and snow, they were fully focused on hay. Number 57 came up to me for a scratch on the nose.

Perhaps it was my imagination, but we all seemed a bit more aware of one another, more appreciative of the warmth and comfort we provided. I felt a rush of relief that we'd weathered the storm and everyone was fine.

Annie and I had much fiddling to do with frozen valves, hauling buckets of water back to the cows as we tried to figure out why the heat tape wasn't working.

Carr, a grumpy farmer, neighbor, and friend from Cossayuna, stopped by to check on me, as he often does, and to offer tips and critiques, many of them quite useful.

"Don't worry about the animals," he declared. "Do you think donkeys and sheep had people like you to bring them cookies and buckets of water five hundred years ago? A storm is nothing to them, just another day."

Maybe so.

Carr figured out the winter water problem years ago, he added. His secret? "I take the hose to bed with me," he said. "I sleep with it. Wrap it around myself and leave one end hanging off the side of the bed, dripping into a bucket. In the morning, I just get up, haul the warm hose outside and screw it in, and the water flows. Never had a problem. My animals always have water, even when it's twenty below."

I silently pondered this approach. The donkeys had gathered around, like spectators at a match, and were listening with intent.

"What does your wife think of your sleeping with a hose?" I asked.

"Don't know," he said, looking surprised. "She never said a thing about it." I chuckled about the hose all day.

As the wind picked up in late afternoon and the temperature began to plunge once again, I walked through the barn, wondering where I had tucked away the summer's hoses, and just how long they were.

Acknowledgments

Acknowledgments can be rote, even ritualistic sometimes, because there are only so many people you can thank, and sometimes you end up thanking the same ones every time.

This book is different.

I really appreciate, and truly need to acknowledge, the people who helped me get it done.

I thank Paula Span. And my daughter, Emma Span, and my sister, Jane Richter.

I appreciate Peggy Trounstine, and the wise counsel, love, and abiding friendship of Steve Draisin and Maria Heinrich. I acknowledge Steve McLean.

I am grateful for Bruce Tracy and Brian McLendon. And for Becky MacLachlan and Mary Kellogg, Ray and Joanne Smith, Annie DiLeo, Melissa Batalin, and Kurtis Albright.

PHOTO: © MARIA HEINRICH

JON KATZ has written eighteen books—six novels and twelve works of nonfiction—including *Izzy & Lenore, Dog Days, A Good Dog, A Dog Year, The Dogs of Bedlam Farm, The New Work of Dogs,* and *Katz on Dogs.* A two-time finalist for the National Magazine Award, he writes columns about dogs and rural life for the online magazine Slate, and has written for *The New York Times, The Wall Street Journal, Rolling Stone, GQ,* and the *AKC Gazette.* Katz is also a photographer, a member of the Association of Pet Dog Trainers, and cohost of the award-winning radio show *Dog Talk* on Northeast Public Radio. He lives on Bedlam Farm in upstate New York with his dogs, sheep, steers and cow, donkeys, barn cat, irritable rooster Winston, and three hens.

www.bedlamfarm.com
www.photosbyjonkatz.com